PROGRAM ANALYSIS FOR STATE AND LOCAL GOVERNMENTS

by Harry Hatry
Louis Blair
Donald Fisk
Wayne Kimmel

The Urban Institute

D0897275

The research forming the basis for this publication was funded by the Office of Policy Development and Research, the Department of Housing and Urban Development, and the Ford Foundation. Opinions expressed are those of the authors and do not necessarily represent the views of The Urban Institute or its sponsors.

Available from:

Publications Office
The Urban Institute
2100 M Street, N.W.
Washington, D.C. 20037

List price: $3.95
Please refer to URI-13700 When Ordering.

Printed in the United States of America

B/77/5M

Foreword

America takes pride in its management techniques. It was long assumed that advances in the management arts, which injected vitality and efficiency into the private sector, would be transferred more or less automatically to the public sector. This has not been the case. State and local officials grappling with their management problems find that business management approaches often lack ready applicability to the special circumstances of government.

Both elective and appointive officials of state and local governments have become increasingly concerned about the high demands placed upon their agencies—whether for dealing with child neglect, waste collection and disposal, air pollution, or crime control.

For half a dozen years The Urban Institute has been cooperating with state and local officials to develop improved management processes for handling these complex problems. This report deals with one of the hurdles that confront many of these officials: how to decide what programs might be best suited to present and future needs. Intuitive approaches, or simply adopting whichever proposals happen to come along, are not satisfactory.

Program analysis is proposed here as a better approach. It involves the systematic appraisal of the likely costs and major effects of feasible alternatives. Its aim is to help officials arrive at appropriate decisions about current and future programs. This report is intended to help state and local governments improve their program analysis capability within their own corridors.

We recognize that program analysis is still in its early stages of development. As states and localities make greater use of the kinds of techniques suggested here, we expect that they will contribute a great deal to the further improvement of these approaches.

William Gorham, President
The Urban Institute

Contents

Exhibits

Preface

Program analysis can be defined readily enough; it is estimating the impacts—especially the costs and effectiveness—of different ways of accomplishing a public purpose.

But going beyond the definition to discover what steps are involved in program analysis, the subject becomes hard to pin down. Program analysis is still more of an art than a science.

There has been little research to validate cost or effectiveness estimation procedures. Seldom have analysts gone back to determine the accuracy of past projections, whether based on elaborate mathematical modeling or on crude, pragmatic procedures. And, of course, it is not possible to verify estimates made for program alternatives that are never tried. Most procedures currently must be accepted either in terms of their apparent logic or on faith.

However, executive and legislative officials must make decisions today on programs affecting the future, usually with very poor information on possible alternatives and their costs and effects. The better the available information, the better the decisions can be.

We hope the material presented here will provide some insights, and at least a few suggestions for improving state and local government program analysis. We also hope that this work will encourage analysts to take steps to improve the art of program analysis.

The reader looking for a detailed, step-by-step "how-to-do-it" book will be disappointed by this volume, for it is impossible in this limited undertaking to define all possible techniques and present examples that apply to many different situations. However, this report does attempt to identify many of the relevant issues and suggest useful approaches for systematic program analysis.

Acknowledgments

The authors wish to express their appreciation to a number of persons who provided valuable comments and suggestions at various stages of this work: George Barbour and Ed Everett, City of Palo Alto, California; Bert Brendle, State of California; James Cavenaugh, State of Pennsylvania; Mark Chadwin, Illinois Economic and Fiscal Commission; Laurence Dougharty and Clarence Teng of the RAND Corporation; Tom Finnie and Robert Horton, Metropolitan Government of Nashville and Davidson County; Jonathan Gaciala, Council of State Governments; Prof. Donald Gross, George Washington University; Gloria Grizzle, State of North Carolina; Douglas Harman and Samuel Finz, County of Fairfax, Virginia; Prof. Kenneth Kraemer, University of California, Irvine; Roger Line, Fort Worth, Texas; James McCullough, Institute for Defense Analyses; Howard McMahon, Oklahoma City, Oklahoma; Fred Patrick, City of Buenaventura, California; Robert Richards, City of Lockport, New York; David L. Smith, County of Santa Barbara, California; Hall Tennis, Michael Gruber, and William Talbert, Metropolitan Dade County, Florida; Chris Tomasides, City-County of Denver, Colorado; and John Hall, Phil Schaenman, and Alfred Schainblatt, The Urban Institute.

H.P.H., L.H.B., D.M.F., W.A.K.

Chapter 1
Program Analysis:
What It's All About

Executive and legislative officials in government have to make difficult decisions about how to use limited resources to meet the needs of the people the government serves. Throughout the year, but particularly at budget time, they have to decide whether to continue an existing program or to adopt new proposals or some alternative to an existing program. Short of guesswork or relying on "the way things have always been done," how should government officials decide?

There is an acute shortage of crystal balls these days, but a more systematic approach to program analysis can help. Program analysis is, in its simplest terms, the systematic, explicit examination of alternative ways to reach public objectives. The process takes in the steps of estimating the future costs, effectiveness, and any other significant impacts of each alternative.

This report attempts to indicate a state and local government personnel how program analysis might help them and describes steps for conducting useful analyses. It concentrates on the types of analysis that a state or local government is most likely to need and will have the capability to undertake. It does not delve into highly technical approaches to analysis; there are many good textbooks on technical procedures, but few basic guides written for state and local government personnel on how to establish, strengthen, or use, a capability for program analysis.

Some Definitions

Let us look more closely at the definition of program analysis by defining certain terms used in this volume.

Costs consist of expenditures of money and other resources, such as manpower, facilities, and land, needed to carry on a program. They include both operating and maintenance expenses and investment expenses, such as for training personnel, constructing facilities, and acquiring land.

Effectiveness is the extent to which a program meets specific goals or objectives. The term also connotes a program's beneficial and detrimental effects on the general public, or on specific parts of that public, called "client groups."

Alternatives are different ways of accomplishing a goal or providing a service. Alternatives can differ by the type of equipment or technology used, by the processes or procedures involved, by the levels of service provided, or by combinations of these.

Techniques of analysis are typically applied to "programs," that is, to government activities or groups of activities that provide direct services to the public, such as crime control, education, health, transportation, recreation, and waste disposal. Program analysis techniques can also be used for analyzing government "support" activities, such as purchasing, finance, and personnel; however, the examples of analysis used in this report are for services to the public rather than for government support services.

A related activity to program analysis is program evaluation. The latter assesses the *past* performance of existing programs. The findings of program evaluations provide important information which is needed for program analysis, since program analysis normally considers an existing program to be one of the alternatives to be examined.[1] Program analysis is essentially focused on *future* activities.

An Illustration of Program Analysis

Examples of the outputs of program analysis and of the steps typically taken to reach those results are presented in Exhibits 1 and 2. Exhibit 1 confronts this problem:[2] County government officials in a northeastern state were concerned about their maternal and infant care

---

[1]Program evaluation is described in a companion report, Harry P. Hatry, Richard E. Winnie, and Donald M. Fisk, *Practical Program Evaluation for State and Local Government Officials* (Washington, D.C.: The Urban Institute, 1973).

[2]This example is adapted from Harry Hatry, "Overview of Modern Program Analysis Characteristics and Techniques" (Washington, D.C.: The Urban Institute, 1969).

Exhibit 1.   ILLUSTRATIVE SUMMARY TABLE:
MATERNAL AND INFANT CARE PROGRAM
ANALYSIS IN A COUNTY

Effectiveness and Costs

Evaluation criteria.	Alternative 1: current program extended	Alternative 2: increased prenatal care emphasis	Alternative 3: increased postnatal care emphasis
1. Annual maternal death rate [a]	0.40	0.36	0.40
2. Annual infant death rate [a]	47	41	47
3. Annual infant defect rate [a]	44	37	27
4. Annual cost	$1,000,000	$1,250,000	$1,200,000

[a] Rates per 1,000 births.

Source: Adapted from Harry Hatry, "Overview of Modern
Program Analysis Characteristics and Techniques"
(Washington, D.C.: The Urban Institute, 1969).

4

Exhibit 2. BASIC STEPS IN A PROGRAM ANALYSIS:
MATERNAL AND INFANT CARE EXAMPLE

1. *Define problem.* What should be done to reduce a high infant mortality rate—relative to the national average—that is occurring in the county hospital?

2. *Identify relevant objectives.* The primary objectives are minimizing maternal mortality and infant mortality and defects.

3. *Select evaluation criteria.* The criteria selected are infant mortality, maternal mortality, infant defects, and program costs.

4. *Specify client groups.* Different client groups identified in this example are mothers and children. Client groups typically have different needs and are served at different levels of effectiveness.

5. *Identify alternatives.* Alternative 1 extends the current program into the future. Alternative 2 has a prenatal care emphasis, including getting expectant mothers into clinics earlier, providing nutrition services, etc. Alternative 3 has a postnatal care emphasis. (The alternatives examined should be specific, potentially operational programs. For example, Alternative 2 might call for the formation of a new clinic of certain size and location, plus a specific type of campaign to publicize the clinic.)

6. *Estimate costs of each alternative.* In Exhibit 1, annual costs could have been shown for each of the next three to five years. They might be presented as either the average annual cost or the total cost over the period.

7. *Determine effectiveness of each alternative.* As shown in Exhibit 1, none of the three alternatives is better than the others for *all* the evaluation criteria. This will happen in most program analyses. Decision makers must now make a judgment using this and other information available to them. Showing the estimated effectiveness of each alternative for each of the next several years would be desirable since the effectiveness of different alternatives might vary.

8. *Presentation of findings.* Exhibit 1 is a tabular method of displaying the estimated costs and effectiveness of alternative programs. In addition to tables, various graphic forms as well as text may be used. (In this simplified example, the amount and nature of the uncertainties in the effectiveness and cost estimates are not indicated but should be presented.)

Note: "Needs assessment" is discussed separately (in Chapter 6). It may be considered as part of the problem definition or as part of the estimation of effectiveness (i.e., estimating the extent to which each alternative meets the "need").

program, in part because the infant mortality rate at the county hospital was higher than the national average. They requested an analysis of the likely costs and effectiveness of alternatives for reducing infant and maternal mortality rates and infant birth defects. Exhibit 1 shows the findings for each of three alternatives which were examined. Exhibit 2 summarizes the steps in the analytic process, which are typical of the basic steps in any program analysis. These steps will be discussed in more detail in Chapters 3 through 6.

Current Status

How often do state and local governments use the kind of systematic program analysis described here? Apparently not very often. Yet governments do conduct many analyses. The following appear to be the most frequent types:

- Cost and revenue analyses;
- Operations or management analyses, usually with emphasis on improving efficiency and reducing costs;
- Economic and population projections; and
- Program evaluations and program audits.

Many local governments and most state governments employ staff members who have the basic capability to perform this type of systematic program analysis, though some may need additional training and guidance. A survey conducted in 1971 by the International City Management Association and The Urban Institute showed that of the 354 cities with more than 50,000 population and counties with more than 100,000 population that responded, 16 percent had central staff units doing "analyses." On the average, these central units devoted about five person-years to analysis activities. The units went under such names as "research," "program analysis," "program planning and evaluation," or "PPBS" (Planning, Programming, Budgeting Systems).[3]

In addition, many of the same city and county governments said some of their operating departments devoted at least half a

---

[3]Richard E. Winnie, "Local Government Budgeting, Program Planning and Evaluation" (Washington, D.C.: International City Management Association, Urban Data Service 4(5), May 1972).

person-year to program planning and evaluation. For example, 25 percent of the governments responding to the survey said their police departments conducted planning and evaluation, as did 12 percent of the transportation agencies and 9 percent of the parks and recreation agencies.

Similarly, 65 percent of the forty-nine state governments responding to a 1974 survey by the National Association of State Budget Officers reported that they had central budget staffs which "conducted program effectiveness analyses."[4] These analyses came into use in making executive budget decisions "to some degree" in twenty-eight states and "to a substantial degree" in another ten states.

The same survey found that central staff agencies performed program effectiveness analysis in ten states, and legislative staffs did so in sixteen states. Operating agencies of eighteen states had "units charged with the conduct of effectiveness or productivity analysis."

The challenge for many cities and counties and a large number of state governments, then, is not only to find people who can perform analysis, but also to make sure that the analysts they already have are doing work that will be most helpful to decision makers. The remainder of this report examines ways to increase the likelihood that program analysis is used effectively and conducted properly.

Contents of the Report

Chapter 2 focuses on the institutional aspects of program analysis. It discusses organizing and staffing for analysis and includes suggestions for selecting issues, scheduling, and reporting findings. Chapters 3 through 7 cover technical aspects of analysis that are of primary interest to staff analysts, but can also be valuable to decision makers by giving them a better perspective on what they should expect from program analysis. Chapter 3 discusses the overall framework for an analysis and some of the first steps in analysis. Chapter 4 discusses the estimation of program costs. Chapter 5 discusses what is probably the most difficult technical issue—the estimation of effectiveness. Chapter 6 presents some miscellaneous

---

[4]National Association of State Budget Officers, "A Survey on the Developments in State Budgeting: A Survey Conducted by the National Association of State Budget Officers' Systems, Techniques and Data Committee" (Lexington, Kentucky, April 1975).

technical topics, such as "needs assessment," the time period to be considered in an analysis, and the handling of uncertainty when estimating cost and effectiveness. Chapter 7 suggests that estimating how feasible an alternative is can be considered part of the program analysis process. This is an aspect that has received little attention in most analyses of governmental programs.

Appendix A present summaries of three actual program analyses, pointing out some of the problems likely to be encountered in a "real world" situation. Appendix B presents two versions of an outline for an "issue paper," suggested in Chapter 2 as a means to begin the analysis process. Appendix C presents a checklist for assessing a program analysis.

Chapter 2
Putting Program Analysis to Work: Institutional Issues

Some of the most sophisticated and technically competent program analyses are unused and unusable. The reasons are varied: the main findings of the analysis may have vanished in a thicket of technical jargon; the recommended alternatives may be politically infeasible; the report on the analysis may have come too late; or the bureaucracy that must use the findings may be uninterested or resistant. In brief, program analysis can be elegant but irrelevant.

To avoid this danger, both the analyst and the public officials who are to use the results of the analysis must pay attention to institutional issues dealing with the ways in which studies are initiated, managed, reviewed, and used. These issues range from the way topics are selected for study to the organization of the analytic staff.

We will start with a fundamental issue: the role of the officials who request a program analysis and who will be primary users of its findings. The comments in this chapter apply primarily to executive officials, both chief executives and department heads, but many should also be of interest to legislative officials.

Role of the Executive and Staff in Program Analysis

Top officials are the people who make decisions, choosing among policy and program alternatives which consume scarce resources both immediately and in the future. These decision makers have a vital interest in getting timely, relevant, and reliable information on the costs and consequences of major decisions. This is what program analyses can help provide.

9

Of course, these officials will not have time to get involved in the details of the analytic process. But such officials can take steps that contribute to the success of program analysis. These steps are listed in Exhibit 3. We will discuss each one here. Officials should:

1. *Participate actively in the selection of program and policy issues for analysis.* There is no substitute for the perspective which a chief executive can bring to the selection of program and policy issues. At a minimum, the executive can usefully screen lists of "candidates" for analysis to eliminate studies of issues which are considered to be trivial or peripheral, and to help ensure that policy questions of greatest concern are considered.

2. *Assign responsibility for the analysis to a unit of the organization which can conduct the study objectively.* If a program analysis cannot be undertaken with reasonable objectivity by the operating agency which will deliver the service, responsibility should be placed in a central staff office or with a multi-agency study team.

3. *Ensure that participation and cooperation are obtained from relevant agencies.* Even when the analysis is assigned to a central unit, staff members of agencies concerned with the issue can contribute significantly to the analysis, and their participation should be obtained whenever possible. Furthermore, their participation can help overcome some of the difficulties associated with implementing a particular alternative. The chief executive can assist an analysis by helping obtain the cooperation of these agencies.

4. *Provide adequate staff to meet a timely reporting schedule.* The effort should be staffed with enough competent people who are allowed sufficient time so that the analysis can be completed and reviewed before a decision has to be made. The chief executive should discourage the diversion of staff from analytical efforts to day-to-day "firefighting."

5. *Insist that the objectives, evaluation criteria, client groups, and program alternatives considered in the analysis include those of prime importance.* The executive should review the study plan early to ensure that it includes these major factors. (The selection of objectives, evaluation criteria, client groups, and alternatives is discussed in Chapter 3.)

11

Exhibit 3.   ROLE OF CHIEF EXECUTIVES
             IN PROGRAM ANALYSIS

1. Participate actively in the selection of program and policy issues for analysis.

2. Assign responsibility for the analysis to a unit of the organization which can conduct the study objectively.

3. Ensure that participation and cooperation are obtained from relevant agencies.

4. Provide adequate staff to meet a timely reporting schedule. schedule.

5. Insist that the objectives, evaluation criteria, client groups, and program alternatives considered in the analysis include those of prime importance.

6. Have a work schedule prepared and periodically monitored.

7. Review results and, if findings seem valid, see that they are used.

6. *Have a work schedule prepared and periodically monitored.* This ensures that interim and final study findings are available in a timely way for key decisions. A member of the executive's staff should be assigned responsibility for monitoring the effort.

7. *Review results, and if findings seem valid, see that they are used.* This helps ensure that program analysis is taken seriously within the organization. It is wise to circulate analysis results to interested agencies to permit reviews and comments before final actions are taken.

Selecting Issues for Analysis

While analytical resources are inevitably scarce, program issues are pervasively abundant. The usual problem is not to find issues but to select those which are most important and which could be clarified significantly by systematic analysis. Some analyses will have to be done on policy problems whose importance emerges because of sudden events; these analyses cannot be scheduled in advance. But generally, waiting for issues to reach a boiling point before undertaking an analysis is likely to prohibit in-depth analysis. State governments and most medium and large local governments will find it useful to have regular, systematic processes to identify issues before they "come to a head" and to select appropriate ones for analysis.

An inexpensive tool for identifying and describing potential topics for analysis is the "issue" or "problem-definition" paper. It describes the major features of a significant problem likely to require government action in the next several months and suggests alternative actions that the government should consider—but stops short of the actual analysis. Two suggested outlines for an issue paper are presented in Appendix B.

The following seven criteria, summarized in Exhibit 4, should help a government select issues and programs for analysis. Criteria 1 through 3 relate to the importance of an issue; Criteria 4 through 7 relate to the feasibility of analysis.

Importance of an Issue

1. *Is there a decision to be made by the government? Can the analysis significantly influence the adoption of various alternatives?* In some instances, key decision makers, such as governors, mayors, city managers, agency heads, legislators, or council members, may have clearly made up their minds. Similarly, strong and controlling interest groups may have already mobilized behind or publicly committed themselves to a single course of action. In such circumstances, the results of analysis will probably have little influence on the final action. However, if there is some suspicion that a course of action has serious defects or major hidden costs and if no decision has been made, a chief executive may wish to proceed with analysis.

2. *Does the issue involve large costs or major consequences for services?* Issues which involve large outlays of resources or hold substantial consequences for the future level, quality, or distribution of public services should receive priority for analysis. Programs that are "analytically interesting" but unlikely to have substantial impact

---

Exhibit 4. CRITERIA FOR SELECTING ISSUES FOR ANALYSIS

Importance of an Issue

1. Is there a decision to be made by the government? Can the analysis significantly influence the adoption of various alternatives?

2. Does the issue involve large costs or major consequences for services?

3. Is there substantial room for improving program performance?

Feasibility of Analysis

4. Can the problem be handled by program analysis?

5. Is there time for the analysis to be done before key decisions must be made?

6. Are personnel and funds available to do the analysis?

7. Do sufficient data exist to undertake the analysis, and can needed data be gathered within the time available?

---

on services or budgets are usually not appropriate topics for program analysis.

3. *Is there substantial room for improving program performance?* If a program is of major importance but there is little room for improving it, examining a program of less "importance" but with more room for improvement may have a higher payoff.

Feasibility of Analysis

4. *Can the problem be handled by program analysis?* Does it lend itself to measurement? Can reasonable estimates of effectiveness be made?

5. *Is there time for the analysis to be done before key decisions must be made?* Program analyses completed and reported *after* officials commit themselves to a course of action can be useless. Studies should consciously be scheduled to allow time for final results and findings to be circulated, reviewed, and evaluated before a decision. It is possible to be too pessimistic about timing, however. A "late" study now may be an early one if the same issue or a comparable one arises again.

6. *Are personnel and funds available to do the analysis?* There is little point in considering analyses which require technical skills that government personnel lack and that cannot be obtained at reasonable costs. Many governments have personnel with most—if not all—necessary analytical skills to undertake a wide range of analyses. In those instances where a technical specialty such as conducting sample surveys is required, outside assistance might be obtained from consulting firms, universities, or research organizations.

7. *Do sufficient data exist to undertake the analysis, and can needed data be gathered within the time available?* Most existing government data records have been designed for administrative, financial, and other control purposes. Few have been designed for measuring and presenting program effectiveness. Even available cost data are often not in a form usable for program cost analyses. Required data, if available at all, may have to be extracted laboriously from existing records or obtained from new sources. Before deciding whether to undertake an analysis, the data that are available should be compared to what will be required; a judgment should be made as to whether available data are adequate, or whether it will be too difficult or expensive to generate new data.

Illustrative Issues for Analysis

Exhibit 5 gives examples of issues which might be selected for analysis. Whether a specific issue contained in the list is worth analyzing depends in part on the application of the seven criteria identified above.

Length and Number of Analyses

The amount of time a study will require should be assessed in advance. Many analyses can be done within three to twelve person-months, but a complex study may require considerably more effort, possibly straining a government's analytical resources. The time required for data collection is often difficult to estimate. Where data are fragmentary, special collection efforts may be necessary. Even with experienced analysts, the time for data *collection* sometimes becomes excessive, at the expense of time for data *analysis*.

How many studies might a government undertake in a given year? This depends in large part on the resources available to do analysis and on the number of "crash" analyses arising. If a government relies primarily on one or two analysts in a central staff, one or two analyses a year may be the limit. If studies are done at the agency level as well, one study a year in each major agency may be taxing, especially where there is no prior experience with program analysis. On the whole, an approach allowing sufficient time to complete assigned analyses is probably more sensible than a broadside approach which attempts more studies and crash analyses than can possibly be finished. The latter approach results in superficiality discrediting the usefulness of analysis in both the short run and the long run. Realism is a necessary antidote to the enthusiasm of those who tend to bite off more analysis than they can chew.

Locating Responsibilities for Program Analysis

There does not appear to be a single best place to locate analytical activities in the government. Variations in the development, experience, and operating style of an organization make varying arrangements appropriate. Some basic points, however, should be considered.

1. *The sole responsibility for analysis should not be put into the hands of individual operating agencies.* Agencies may be tempted to give priority consideration only to alternatives or policy actions which are in their self-interest, and which tend to continue their current ways of operation. Operating agencies may overlook effects and impacts beyond their scope of interest or responsibility. Single-agency analyses may define problems too narrowly or employ restricted alternatives and criteria. For example, a police agency might not give full consideration to the disposition of arrests; traffic control agencies might neglect the air and noise pollution spillovers of their programs;

Exhibit 5. ILLUSTRATIVE ISSUES FOR PROGRAM ANALYSIS

Law Enforcement

1. What is the most effective way of distributing limited police forces—by time of day, day of week, and geographical location?

2. What types of police units (foot patrolmen, one- or two-man police cars, special task forces, canine corps units, or others) should be used and in what mix?

3. What types of equipment (considering both current and new technologies) should be used for weaponry, for communications, and for transportation?

4. How can the judicial process be improved to provide more expeditious service, keep potentially dangerous persons from running loose, and at the same time protect the rights of the innocent?

5. How can criminal detection institutions be improved to maximize the probability of rehabilitation, while remaining a deterrent to further crime?

Fire Protection

1. Where should fire stations be located, and how many are needed?

2. How should firefighting units be deployed, and how large should units be?

3. What types of equipment should be used for communications, transportation, and firefighting?

4. Are there fire prevention activities, such as inspection of potential fire hazards or school educational programs, that can be used effectively?

Health and Social Services

1. What mix of treatment programs should do the most to meet the needs of the expected mix of clients?

2. What prevention programs are desirable for the groups that seem most likely to suffer particular ailments?

Exhibit 5. (continued)   17

Housing

1. To what extent can housing code enforcement programs be used to decrease the number of families living in substandard housing? Will such programs have an adverse effect on the overall supply of low-income housing in the community?

2. What is the appropriate mix of code enforcement with other housing programs to make housing in the community adequate?

3. What is the best mix of housing rehabilitation, housing maintenance, and new construction to improve the quantity and quality of housing?

Employment

1. What relative support should be given to training and employment programs which serve different client groups?

2. What should be the mix among outreach programs, training programs, job-finding and matching programs, antidiscrimination programs, and post-employment follow-up programs?

Waste

1. How should waste be collected and disposed of, given alternative visual, air, water, and pollution standards?

2. What specific equipment and routings should be used?

Recreation and Leisure

1. What type, location, and size of recreation facilities should be provided for those desiring them?

2. How should recreation facilities be divided among summer and winter, daytime and nighttime, and indoor and outdoor activities?

3. What, and how many, special summer programs should be made available for out-of-school youths?

4. What charges, if any, should be made to users, considering such factors as differential usage and ability to pay?

housing authorities might be more interested in enlarging the stock of community housing than maintaining what exists in a liveable condition. It is unlikely, for instance, that a single operating agency would have had adequate perspective to undertake the analysis of drug abuse treatment programs described in Appendix A-3.

A unit *outside or above* an operating program should direct, participate in, or at least monitor analyses. In all states and in local jurisdictions with more than about 100,000 population, at least a small central staff for program analysis and the allied functions of evaluation, program planning, and research is probably desirable. A central staff can itself conduct analyses with participation from operating agencies and possibly outside consultants; stimulate, monitor, and review agency-level studies; and provide such agency studies with technical assistance. In smaller jurisdictions, where a full-time central program analysis staff may not be feasible, these functions could be carried out part-time by one or two staff members in the chief executive's office or budget office who do not have direct operating responsibilities.

In addition to a central staff, there are often analytic capabilities available at the agency level in states and in larger jurisdictions. The report of the survey of local governments conducted jointly by the International City Management Association and The Urban Institute indicated that, especially in cities over 100,000 population, small staffs already exist, particularly in some major agencies.[1] However, some units, such as police planning and research units, are often engaged primarily in gathering and tabulating statistics. Except in the very largest cities, such units typically do little full-fledged program analysis or evaluation. These units can serve, nonetheless, as the nucleus for building an agency's analytical capability. Many state governments have analysis and/or evaluation staffs in some of their larger agencies.

2. *Analysts should have access and be exposed to the needs and policy views of key decision makers.* The central staff performing analyses should probably report directly to the chief executive or to a principal advisor. Analyses are then more likely to reflect managerial and political realities.

---

[1]Richard E. Winnie, "Local Government Budgeting, Program Planning, and Evaluation" (Washington, D.C.: The International City Management Association, Urban Data Service 4(5), May 1972), Table 7.

3. *The time spent by analysts on daily "firefighting" operations should be limited.* The demands for responses to daily issues are unending and can inhibit or even prevent in-depth examination of issues. Analysts should be in touch with the dynamics of policy making, but should not be swamped with daily rush jobs.

4. *An analysis unit should probably maintain a close relationship with the budget office.* The budget office often has a strong voice in implementing the results of an analysis. Some governments have tried to make budget examiners into part-time program analysts or to give new program analysts some regular budgetary responsibilities. While appealing in principle, this arrangement sometimes creates difficulties, at least initially, because the routine burdens of budget administration require so much time.

Analysts and the budget staff can, of course, interact during the course of a study. Budget staff members can, for example, advise the analysis team on costs of alternatives. It may be possible to merge the budget staff with the analysis staff once a tradition of analysis has been established and accepted. But experience to date suggests that initially the program analysis staff should be separate.

5. *The functions of program evaluation and program analysis can be placed in the same office.* Program evaluation—the assessment of how existing programs have performed in the past—provides basic information for program analysis. Past performance can be projected into the future as part of the task of assessing alternatives. Similar, if not identical, skills are needed for the two functions. It may be economical to combine the two in an "Office of Program Evaluation and Analysis." But care should be taken to avoid the pressures to evaluate a program favorably because it resulted from a previous analysis conducted by the same office.

A Special Note: Use Agency Staff in the Analysis

Many staff members of operating agencies concerned with the issue being analyzed are experts in their fields. Analysts who are not already familiar with the field should draw on their expertise. The agency experts should certainly be members of an analysis "team," in cases where a team is used. Participation of experienced staff members from operating agencies and their contact with analysts will not only yield more complete, reliable, and relevant information, but will also increase the likelihood that the agency will cooperate in implementing the recommendations that result from the study.

Staff Skills and Training

To perform most analyses, an individual does not need extensive training in a major professional speciality. What an analyst needs is intelligence and an inquiring, systematic, analytical approach to solving problems. Many governments already employ staff members who with proper direction could successfully undertake program and policy analyses. Other staff members could qualify with training and experience. Nonetheless, there is a shortage of individuals with actual experience and training in program analysis.

Quantitative training in such fields as economics, engineering, or operations research does give some advantage to potential analysts because several of the premises (e.g., the widespread scarcity of resources), approaches (e.g., routinely considering alternatives), and techniques (e.g., use of quantititave data) associated with program analysis are familiar to persons with these disciplines. But high-quality analytical work can be performed by staff members without these specialized backgrounds.

A look at the composition of specific analytic staffs is instructive. To complement a cadre of economists, the U.S. Department of Health, Education, and Welfare recruited individuals with a broad range of skills and experiences. This staff produced a number of useful studies, including one on maternal and child health directed by an analytical philosopher and one on health services for the poor led by a young medical doctor.

Reflecting on analytical work in the Department of Defense, economist Charles Hitch (later president of the University of California) said:

It is my experience that the hardest problems for the systems analyst are not those of analytical techniques. In fact, the techniques we use in the Office of the Secretary of Defense are usually rather simple and old-fashioned. What distinguishes the useful and productive analyst is his ability to formulate (or design) the problem; to choose appropriate objectives; to define the relevant, important environments or situations in which to test the alternatives; to judge the reliability of his cost and other data; and finally, and not least, his ingenuity in inventing new systems or alternatives to evaluate.[2]

A larger future supply of trained analysts seems likely as graduate schools of public and business administration, public affairs, and policy analysis provide more exposure to quantitative subjects. Graduates in engineering, operations research, and economics are showing increasing interest in employment in state and local government, and some personnel with appropriate analytical experience in the aerospace industries are increasingly available to state and local governments. All such people are prime candidates for positions as analysts, provided they have the right kind of inquiring, systematic frame of mind and some guidance from experienced project leaders.

Perhaps the major gap in the near future will be a shortage of program analysis project leaders who can provide direction, guidance, and on-the-job training to inexperienced personnel.

Use of Outside Resources

Analytical projects sometimes require special skills and personnel resources that are not available within a government. This is likely to occur where an analysis staff is small or when the analysis requires an "exotic" skill or speciality. Services of consulting firms, universities, and research organizations can be hired to augment existing skills.

Accessible, and sometimes inexpensive, technical resources for state and local governments may exist in nearby colleges and universities. Users should be albert, however, that some academics prefer to work on federal-level problems, may be inclined toward ivory tower solutions, or may emphasize work that is publishable from a disciplinary perspective rather than practical for the government. Yet, new incentives are emerging for universities to get involved in state and local government. Schools of public affairs and policy analysis that are oriented to "messy" and "lower-level" practical problems are evolving. College students also seem more eager to

---

[2]Charles J. Hitch, *Decision Making for Defense* (Berkeley and Los Angeles: University of California Press, 1965), p. 54.

participate in "real world" studies, and some institutions give credit for work-study projects. Policy studies may give students an opportunity to work with data which are not in the library.

Federal government agencies, business firms, and even private civic groups such as the local League of Women Voters and chamber of commerce are sometimes potential sources of help. Both profit-making and nonprofit firms may be willing to participate in an analysis as a public service, for the sake of the learning experience, to test out or share some of their own technology, or simply to make contacts for possible future business.

Here are some examples of cooperation from outside organizations:

• As part of a cooperative effort with the city of East Lansing, Michigan, the National Bureau of Standards (NBS) loaned two technical staffers to work on an analysis of the location of new fire stations. The analysts used a component of an existing computer model which had been developed by NBS. The Bureau experts participated in a productive user-technician dialogue with city officials. Based on the success of the computer model, the city planned to use it in the analysis of several other city problems to which it appears applicable.[3]

• New York City undertook a study of the effectiveness of emergency ambulance services. Shortly after the study began, a large computer firm undertook development of a computer simulation of ambulance services. The model was used in the analysis to calculate "response times" for three alternative modes of deploying ambulances. The firm did not charge the city for the use of the model. The analyst who developed it later joined the analysis staff of the city.[4]

• The Leagues of Women Voters of both Arlington County, Virginia and Randolph Township, New Jersey have provided

---

[3]Marvin R. Burt, Donald M. Fisk, and Harry P. Hatry, "Factors Affecting the Impact of Urban Policy Analysis: Ten Case Histories," Working Paper 201-3 (Washington, D.C.: The Urban Institute, July 1972), pp. 20-21.

[4]Ibid., pp. 56-63.

volunteer interviewers to their local governments for surveys of citizen experience with local government services. Similarly, the Birmingham, Alabama Health and Welfare (community services) Council assisted the city with a survey of citizen views of recreation needs and performance.

In addition to obtaining assistance with part of an analysis, a government may use an outside group, such as a consulting firm, to conduct an entire program analysis. This may be required when internal staff resources are already committed, when the analysis is beyond their capability, or when a firm might bring greater "credibility" or "impartiality" to a controversial study. In these instances, governments ought to keep in mind four caveats:

1. Study costs are likely to be higher than those of an analysis conducted internally.

2. An outside group may not have or be able to acquire in the available time an adequate perspective of a complex policy problem.

3. An outside firm may be perceived as a greater threat than an internal group and perhaps find less cooperation, though in some instances the reverse may be true.

4. Implementing outside findings may not be as palatable to those inside who have to live with the consequences of recommendations which were "invented" elsewhere. Thus, although outside studies may be of higher technical quality, they may present problems when the time comes to implement their recommendations.

To improve the quality and usefulness of analyses conducted from outside, the following may be helpful:

1. *The government should be as clear as possible about what problem or problems it is asking an outside group to study.* While most problems are clarified and sometimes transformed in the very course of analysis, many studies miss their mark—and disappoint their clients—because the government really had no idea what it wanted in the first place.

2. Before much effort has been expended, the government should review and discuss the plan to be followed with the contractor. This includes defining and reaching an understanding of the issues or problems to be addressed, listing the major alternatives to be examined, identifying the principal criteria of effectiveness to be employed, specifying the target populations to be considered, and defining the general scope and methodology to be employed.

3. Periodic and intensive meetings should be held during the study, especially in the early stages, to ensure communication on the subject and progress of the analysis. A government project monitor should be assigned to each study contract.

4. The government should specify the type and amount of staff assistance and data it will provide. It should ensure that the contractor has reasonable and effective access to the agencies and personnel from which information is to be obtained.

5. The government should offer a clear understanding of the products it wants, including interim and final reports, and the schedule on which the products are to be delivered. Findings which are too late for use in decisions are often useless. Regular written progress reports are valuable to both parties. Final reports should be in writing and accompanied by oral briefings and interpretations. The major assumptions and procedures of the study as well as the findings should be explicitly stated and documented. The data used in the study should be provided to the government in an understandable form.

Presentation of Results

If the specific findings and implications of an analysis cannot be readily understood they are not likely to be used. Even the best analysis will be ignored or rejected if it appears to be esoteric, sloppy, rambling, or incoherent. Analysts have to communicate their findings clearly to decision makers interested in very specific matters. Some decision makers prefer oral presentations; others prefer written reports. Either way, most public officials lack the time or specialized training to pore over lengthy technical arguments, long tables, computer printouts, or formulas to discover what an analysis has found. The analysts' job is to present their findings in a comprehensible way—in clear English and in a compact and orderly fashion. Some guidelines that can make an analysis more comprehensible and meaningful are:

1. *Before distributing an analysis, have it reviewed.* A review of the draft by program people and one or two good technicians not involved in the analysis may turn up important omissions, errors, misinterpretations of data, faulty methods, bad logic, or unsubstantiated conclusions. The review can also reveal important points of debate or controversy. It is often reasonable to discuss major objections and responses to the report's recommendations in the report itself.

2. *Present findings in writing.* This will reduce the possibility of misunderstanding and permit an analysis to be reviewed as explained above. Even though decision makers may not want to read the report or have time to do so, the document should be available for review by staff.

3. *Present a compact, clear summary.* The technical details of a study may thrill an analyst but bore a busy official. These details should be included in the body of a report or in appendices, but no reader should have to wade through minutiae to reach the findings.

4. *Acknowledge the limitations and assumptions of a study.* State them explicitly. Do not force a decision maker to sniff them out. For objective analysis, the presentation should include all sides of the story: the good, the bad, and the unknown. For example, in the case of the Fort Worth car plan analysis (see Appendix A-2), the city attorney indicated that he felt that the plan violated the state constitution. This was reported in the analysis but it was also pointed out that at least two other cities in the state had already started to use a similar plan.

5. *Use simple graphics where possible to communicate major findings and conclusions.* A "picture"—if it is a good one—is still worth a thousand words.

6. *Get rid of jargon.* Have one or two laymen read the body of the study to see if it is understandable.[5]

7. *Tailor the presentation to the decision maker who will use it.* Some may prefer tables, other graphs. Some will demand one-page executive summaries. Others will want to have all the details. Some will want special oral briefings, others will not.

Cost of Program Analysis

Program analysis is not free. Costs of individual studies vary widely, depending on such factors as the length of the study, the complexity of the issue, the size of the analytical team employed, the cost of data collection, and charges for outside help. Major program analyses, such as those at the federal level, have cost several hundred thousand dollars. Analyses for state and local governments, of the type discussed in this report, are likely to average three to twelve person-months of analytical effort. Extended studies may require two to three person-years.

One way to put the costs of program analyses into perspective is to relate them to the costs associated with the programs under study. Over the last several years the federal government has earmarked anywhere from 0.5 to 2 percent of total program costs for analysis and evaluation. This is well above the amount currently being spent by most state and local governments.

Here are a few illustrations of the variations of costs or analysts' time spent in conducting several program analyses: [6]

• A study of the size and deployment of the fireboat fleet of a large eastern city took an analyst three weeks plus an undetermined amount of time for data collection by the fire department. The potential costs associated with the policy issue under study ranged from $500,000 to $1.5 million.

---

[5]Useful books to help technical writers write clearly are Rudolf Flesch, *The Art of Readable Writing* (New York: Harper and Row, 1949); Robert Gunning, *The Technique of Clear Writing* (New York: McGraw-Hill, 1968).

[6]Marvin R. Burt, Donald M. Fisk, and Harry P. Hatry, "Factors Affecting the Impact of Urban Policy Analysis: Ten case Histories," Working Paper 201-3 (Washington, D.C.: The Urban Institute, July 1972); and International City Management Association, "Applying Systems Analysis in Local Government: Three Case Studies" (Washington, D.C., 1972).

• An analysis of the need for and location of two new fire stations cost approximately $20,000 including direct city costs, outside technical assistance, and computer costs. The issue under study was whether to spend $500,000 in new capital and $130,000 in new annual operating costs to build two new fire stations.

• A senior analyst spent four months analyzing alternative ways of improving onsite trash incineration to meet minimum legal air pollution standards. The alternatives under study entailed a combined cost to the city and landlords ranging from $56 million to $404 million.

• An assessment of alternatives for reducing response times of emergency ambulance services in a large city took about one person-year and cost the city more than $100,000. The additional cost of developing and running a computer model was absorbed by an information systems firm.

Whether a study is worth it is a relative consideration; there are no absolute rules. Program analyses can result not only in cost savings but also improvements in program effectiveness and public services. The latter may far outweigh in importance the direct budgetary costs of a study.

Factors Affecting the Impact of Analysis

Why do some program analyses appear to have substantial impact on the decisions of public officials, while others have very little or are ignored? A number of factors beyond a study's technical sophistication affect its impact. There is no systematic evidence to pinpoint all of them.

However, a review of several case studies can tell us about some of the apparent hallmarks of study success, failure, and impact on policy. The Urban Institute examined in some detail the history and characteristics of ten documented program analyses conducted by local governments in 1968 and 1969.[7] Although the results are merely

---

[7]The material in the remainder of this section is based on Burt, *et al.*, op. cit.

suggestive and not definitive because of the small number of cases, they are worth considering.

The ten cases examined are listed in Exhibit 6. The first five dealt with problems of where resources should be located in the city. All these cases employed some version of operations research or mathematical modeling techniques. The scope of these five studies was kept fairly narrow. Broad or "total" system analysis was not attempted. The remaining five cases dealt with larger "system" aspects of problems and, in general, considered a wider range of program alternatives.

The researchers judged the impact of each study on policy. Two categories were used: "considerable or moderate" and "slight or none." Of the ten cases, six were judged to have only slight or no impact, while the other four appeared to have a greater impact.

Ten factors, listed in Exhibit 7, were considered to have potential effects on the impact of analyses on policy. Five were "technical," including the type of problem analyzed and the method employed. The other five were "bureaucratic" variables, such as the level of a decision maker's interest in an analysis and whether or not the results of the analysis implied changes in the money to be spent for a program. In each of the ten cases, the researchers judged how the ten factors related to the impact that the analysis had on policy.

Three of the five "technical" factors examined appeared to have the strongest relationships to impact. The analyses which influenced decisions were those which:

1. Were well-timed, so that study findings were available at key decision points.

2. Included an explicit consideration of political and administrative issues which might affect the implementation of study findings.

3. Focused on well-defined problems rather than on broad or open-ended ones.

The size of the study and the adequacy of its methods seemed to be less clearly related to the study's impact.

Two of the "bureaucratic" variables examined appeared to have strong relationships to impact. The analyses which affected policy dealt with issues which could not be deferred by policy makers and focused on issues in which decision makers had shown clear interest.

Exhibit 6. TEN CASE HISTORIES

1. *Fireboat A* examined the existing fireboats and various alternatives as to their type, number, and location for controlling fires near or on the waterfront.

2. *Fireboat B* examined the desirable number and location of fireboats for controlling fires on or near the waterfront.

3. *Fire Station Location* examined the question of how many fire stations there should be and where they should be located to provide fire protection.

4. *Emergency Ambulance Service* examined the number and location of ambulances needed to provide the fastest response to emergency calls.

5. *Mechanical Street Sweeping* examined the best way to allocate existing mechanical sweeping resources to maximize their effectiveness—with limited augmentation of resources as a possible option.

6. *Onsite Incineration* examined various ways of meeting new minimum air pollution standards regarding incinerators in both public and private apartment buildings, including enforcement of penalties to require upgrading of incinerators and the consequences to hauling requirements where incinerators were shut down.

7. *Solid Waste Collection and Disposal* examined a wide spectrum of collection and disposal options, including curbside versus backyard collection, various alternatives for solid waste containers, and a sanitary landfill versus incineration for solid waste disposal.

8. *Swimming Opportunities* examined various alternatives for providing swimming opportunities for the residents of a Model Cities neighborhood, including various numbers and sizes of pools and busing to a nearby oceanfront beach.

9. *Subemployment* examined how unemployment and underemployment might be reduced in the city's Model Cities neighborhood. The emphasis was on determining the effectiveness of existing manpower training programs and placement agencies.

10. *Venereal Disease Control* examined the problem of reducing the prevalence of gonorrhea and syphilis, with emphasis on gonorrhea.

Source: Burt, *et al., op. cit.*

Whether an analysis proposed changes in a program's funding level and whether agency members who would have to implement study recommendations actually participated in the study did not seem to be related significantly to the impact of analysis in these cases.

Some of the findings of this study tend to support intuitive feelings. For example, it is common sense that a study will have more impact if it is well timed, holds a decision maker's interest, and takes into account the administrative and political feasibility of implementing recommendations.

Effects of Limited Time and Resources: "Quickie" Analysis

There will be many times in state and local governments when a program analysis is needed but time and staffing to undertake it are limited. Unfortunately, the "quickie" or "crash" analysis may be the most common method for most governments. Under these circumstances, it will probably be necessary to limit the number of alternatives considered; to use data that are currently, or at least quickly, available; and to do a less comprehensive and thorough analysis.

Of course, any such shortcuts will weaken the analysis, and this should be specifically noted in the analysis report. But even "quickie" studies should apply the basic analytical principles and tools discussed in Chapters 3 through 6. Limited time and resources are no excuse for neglecting the basics.

After the Analysis: Implementation and Follow-up

Analysis helps bring policy makers *to* decisions. But what should be done *after* a decision is made to implement a new program or modify an old one? Chapter 7 considers some ways analysts can increase the practicality of their analyses. Executives and analysts should consider the following approaches as well:

1. The executive might assign to staff members (perhaps even from the program analysis staff) responsibility for following the implementation process. Such staff should develop a schedule for implementation, and monitor the progress and report if the process breaks down. Should problems arise or delays occur, early detection helps ensure that accountability for implementing changes is established.

Exhibit 7. FACTORS EXAMINED FOR THEIR INFLUENCE ON
THE IMPACT OF ANALYSIS

Technical Variables

1. Study size

2. Study timing

3. Methodological adequacy

4. Consideration of implementation

5. Nature of problem studied

Bureaucratic and Political Variables

6. Decision maker interest

7. Implementer's participation

8. Single-agency issue

9. Proposed changes in funding

10. Immediate decision needed.

Source: Burt, *el al.,* op. cit.

2. An evaluation of an implemented program might be conducted after it has been in operation for a reasonable amount of time—both to gather information to help with future decisions and to gain feedback about the accuracy of projections analysts made. This can help analysts make improvements in their analysis. It is also a way to hold program analysts accountable for their work and to assess the program analysis process itself.

Limitations and Dangers of Analysis

Analysis can provide a decision maker with information to use in making a difficult decision, but it rarely points to a single best alternative. The decision maker will have to weigh the trade-offs, costs, and differing effects on various client groups that the analysis identifies for each alternative. Analysis does not inherently complicate decision making; it simply identifies complications that already exist and attempts to provide information to help the decision maker handle them.

Both decision makers and analysts should guard against the following tendencies:

1. Concentrating on aspects of a problem that are easy to measure while downplaying other aspects that are more difficult to measure but just as vital.

2. Becoming so fascinated with sophisticated mathematical techniques that time and money are drained from other considerations. Sometimes simple, commonplace techniques are perfectly adequate for gathering the necessary information. In such cases, resources given to constructing an elaborate computer-based model, for example, are wasted.

3. Delaying decisions to perform more analysis for its own sake. From a technical viewpoint, it may frequently be desirable to wait for a more definitive analysis, but this must be balanced against the sometimes urgent need to make a decision.

Chapter 3
Improving on Crystal Ball Gazing: The Basic Elements of Program Analysis

The previous chapter emphasized the roles and responsibilities of decision makers in carrying out successful program analyses. Even with the support of decision makers, program analysis is still fraught with difficulties. The remaining chapters are devoted to aiding the analyst in conducting the basic steps of program analysis. See Exhibit 2 for a list of typical steps. While the elements are presented as a series of steps, actual analysis usually involves an interplay among the steps, such as backtracking to refine or redefine the problem, to specify additional client groups, or to pose additional evaluation criteria.

This chapter discusses the first five steps: defining the problem, identifying objectives, selecting evaluation criteria, specifying client groups, and identifying alternatives. In considering the suggestions in Chapters 3 through 6, it may be helpful to refer to the three examples of analyses summarized in Appendix A, and the checklist of technical criteria for assessing program analyses in Appendix C.

Defining the Problem and Its Scope

Program analysis starts with a given problem. The following examples from Appendix A illustrate the nature of such problems as they were initially proposed:

1. Nashville mayor's office: Do we need to build three new cottages at our Children's Home, as has been proposed?

2. Fort Worth City Council: *Parade Magazine* says that Indianapolis lets their police officers drive their patrol cars while off duty, and as a result the crime rate has dropped substantially. Should we do the same?

3. Dade County manager: What drug treatment program should the county encourage and support?

An analyst should, of course, respond to a problem or issue as it is initially perceived by government officials. But beyond that, analysts should attempt to identify the "real" problem which may underlie a given issue. As initially posed, a problem may be stated vaguely, incompletely, or perhaps misleadingly. Analysts will neglect part of their job if they indiscriminately accept the characterization of a problem as it is first and roughly presented. But problems and issues should not be redefined or reformulated merely to suit the analyst or to fit his analytic tools. Significant changes in problem statements should be worked out with, or reviewed by, responsible officials before the study is well under way.

One of the first problems that an analyst will normally face is determining the scope of an analysis. Should it focus on very narrow aspects of a problem or should it encompass numerous and broad dimensions? The analysis of the Fort Worth take-home police car plan, for example, focused on a very narrow issue. It considered only the existing use of police cars in Fort Worth and the variations of the basic take-home plan used in Indianapolis. The analysts might have explored other possible ways to reduce crimes, such as providing additional police officers or improving street lighting. The analysis could also have included additional options such as one-officer versus two-officer patrol cars or uniformed versus nonuniformed patrol officers. It could have been expanded to include the role of courts and prisons in deterring and apprehending criminals. The scope could have been further widened to consider the role of education, employment, and welfare in preventing crime in the first place. In fact, the scope was defined narrowly because of the specific interests of the city manager and council at the time.

The scope will be determined by such factors as the resources and time available, the amount of information that is available or that can be developed in time, and the interests and needs of the government. But even within these limitations an analyst will usually have some flexibility in defining the scope. In practice, there is a common tendency to define a problem too narrowly. For example, an analysis of emergency ambulance service was criticized for concentrating excessively on the response time of the ambulances. It had little to say either about provisions for medical care after arrival at the scene or hospital or about the relation of response time to health.

Conversely, an analysis may define an issue too broadly by attempting to answer all possible questions with one study which is so large and so difficult that it cannot be completed within the time and funding available. The choice of scope should be based in part on a preliminary analysis of a problem to help assess where analysts' time and effort would probably provide the largest payoff. An issue paper of the type described in Chapter 2 and Appendix B is one way to do this. Such preliminary analysis is seldom undertaken, unfortunately.

The initial scope of a study may be altered during the course of analysis, especially if important new insights about a problem arise. For example, the drug abuse treatment analysis summarized in Appendix A-3 was broadened during the actual study to include the county jail when it became apparent that the jail was a major potential source of clients for treatment. As a general practice, the approximate scope of analysis should be defined at an early stage by the analysts and then reviewed by appropriate officials before a great deal of effort is expended.

One tool sometimes useful for gaining perspective on the scope of an issue is "diagramming" the service delivery system under study. This technique can help indicate how the elements of a system relate to each other and guide the selection of factors that should be considered in the analysis. Exhibit 8 is an illustration of one form of diagram. This exhibit shows various levels of a health treatment system. Each block represents a segment of the total population served by the system. If data were obtained on the number of cases falling into each block, the information could help identify those elements that are deficient and thus have priority for examination in a program analysis.

36

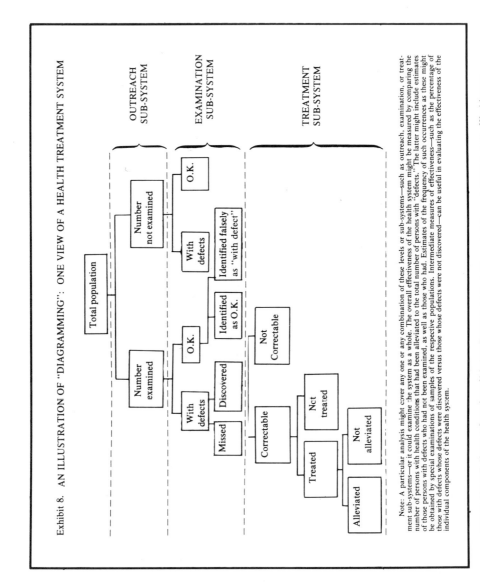

Exhibit 8. AN ILLUSTRATION OF "DIAGRAMMING": ONE VIEW OF A HEALTH TREATMENT SYSTEM

Note: A particular analysis might cover any one or any combination of these levels or sub-systems—such as outreach, examination, or treatment sub-systems—or it could examine the system as a whole. The overall effectiveness of the health system might be measured by comparing the number of persons with health conditions that had been alleviated to the total number of persons with "defects." The latter might include estimates of those persons with defects who had not been examined, as well as those who had. Estimates of the frequency of such occurrences as these might be obtained by special examinations of samples of the respective populations. Intermediate measures of effectiveness—such as the percentage of those with defects whose defects were discovered versus those whose defects were not discovered—can be useful in evaluating the effectiveness of the individual components of the health system.

Source: Harry P. Hatry, "Overview of Modern Program Analysis Characteristics and Techniques" (Washington, D.C.: The Urban Institute, 1969).

Identifying Program Objectives, Evaluation Criteria, and Client Groups

Three essential steps in program analysis are identifying relevant program objectives, criteria by which to evaluate the effectiveness of alternatives ("measures of effectiveness"), and the population or client groups which will be affected by the alternatives. These steps are closely related and will be discussed together. In practice, they can and probably should be undertaken jointly.

Whenever possible, officials who request a program analysis should review the objectives, measures, and client groups selected by the analysts before data gathering begins. This will help ensure that the coverage of the analysis is appropriate.

The terms "objectives" and "goals" refer to the purposes of a government service. An objective or goal can be a desirable result that should be maximized, or an undesirable effect that should be minimized. Some writers distinguish between goals and objectives, but we make no such distinction in this volume.

Evaluation criteria, or measures of effectiveness, are criteria that indicate the extent to which the program is achieving its objectives.

Client groups are considered to be population groups that a program is intentionally directed toward, or groups that the program unintentionally affects.

Some suggestions for carrying out these three steps of program analysis follow:

1. *Identify objectives and evalution criteria that are people-oriented.* Objectives and the evaluation criteria associated with them should reflect potential impacts on citizens and the community. Evaluation criteria should help address the question, "How well is the service doing what it should do for the citizens who use or are affected by it?" Exhibit 9 lists some characteristics of services that such criteria should address.

Objectives and evaluation criteria should cover the public conditions that a program is designed to maintain, achieve or change. For example, criteria should measure how well a program meets the objectives of increasing the health and safety of citizens, or the cleanliness of the streets, or the satisfaction of citizens with the quality and variety of recreational opportunities.

Exhibit 9.   CHARACTERISTICS THAT EVALUATION
CRITERIA SHOULD ADDRESS

1.   To what degree does the service meet its intended purposes, such as improving health, reducing crime, or increasing employment?

2.   To what degree does the program have unintended adverse or beneficial impacts? For example, does a new industry increase water and air pollution or cause inconvenience to citizens?

3.   Is the quantity of the service provided sufficient to meet the needs and desires of citizens? What percent of the eligible "needy" population is actually served?

4.   How fast does the program respond to requests for service?

5.   Do government employees treat citizens who use the service with courtesy and dignity?

6.   How accessible is the service to users?

7.   Do citizens who use the service, or who might use the service, view it as satisfactory?

8.   How much does the program cost?

Unfortunately, there is a widespread tendency to concentrate either on workload measures, such as tons of garbage collected, number of cases handled, or number of persons processed at intake; or on immediately available physical measures, such as number of acres of playground or number of hospital beds. While these measures may be useful for indicating some aspects of program performance, they provide little information about the extent to which citizens and the community are served effectively.

2. *Explicitly consider potential "unintended" consequences of programs—particularly negative effects.* For example:

- Major new road building programs may result in displacement of large numbers of citizens, noise and air pollution, and disruption of the community.
- Urban renewal or housing code enforcement programs may reduce the amount of low-income housing available in a community.
- Increased arrest activities by public safety officials could, without proper safeguards cause undue citizen harassment.
- New solid waste disposal technology may cause objectionable amounts of air or noise pollution.

The key point here—one that is often neglected—is that an explicit objective should be to control a program's negative consequences. Objectives are usually expressed as the beneficial effects that are intended but most programs also have negative consequences. Each program alternative should be examined to assess possible side-effects, both beneficial and harmful. Explicit consideration of negative consequences will help put the overall worth of a program into proper perspective and help governments design programs that reduce negative consequences.

3. *Consider more than one objective and evaluation criterion.* Most programs will have several purposes, some of which may be interdependent or even conflicting. A single objective will rarely describe adequately the effect of the program, nor will a single evaluation criterion fully measure its impact. Some of the many aspects of a program which may need to be covered by evaluation

criteria were listed in Exhibit 9. Exhibits 10 and 11 illustrate evaluation criteria from two program analyses summarized in Appendix A.[1]

4. *Don't reject evaluation criteria because of apparent difficulties in measuring them.* Evaluation criteria should be identified without initial concern for how or whether they can be measured. There are generally ways to partially measure even qualitative, subjective criteria, for example, by estimates based on ratings by experts or on systematic surveys of former clients. In any case, analysts should identify evaluation criteria even where they can provide no information to measure them. This will help ensure that decision makers using an analysis will be aware of important omissions and will remember to consider those aspects which are relevant but not yet measured.

5. *Too many objectives or criteria are better than too few.* It is probably better to err initially on the side of including too many objectives or evaluation criteria for consideration than to eliminate some that might be important when examined more closely. Neither public officials nor program analysts should be quick to eliminate a potential evaluation criterion on the basis of their own personal opinion. Criteria that become irrelevant or insignificant during the course of an analysis can be discarded, but it is often difficult to introduce new ones midway in the process without repeating data collection efforts.

6. *Specify client groups on which the analysis should attempt to estimate program impacts.* A program usually affects different groups in different ways and to different degrees. An analysis should identify these groups and collect information on how the program will affect them. For example, the average crime rate or average family income for a jurisdiction masks differences among subgroups of a population. The following points should be considered:

- Each program will be directed toward some groups that are *intended* beneficiaries (clients) of the service.

---

[1]These are not presented as examples of perfect objectives or evaluation criteria but only as reasonable ones that appeared to have been relevant, reasonably comprehensive, and useful for the analyses in which they were applied.

Exhibit 10   ILLUSTRATION OF OBJECTIVES AND
EVALUATION CRITERIA: NASHVILLE
NEGLECTED AND DEPENDENT CHILDREN
PROGRAM ANALYSIS

Objectives

A. Reduce the number of neglected and dependent (N-D) petitions filed
and the number of children subjected to the system by screening out
those cases in which a petition is not justified.

B. Keep the child in his or her home or in a family environment when
possible until a thorough study can be conducted and the disposition
of the case is decided. Seek to avoid institutional placements.

C. Keep the child in his or her home or an appropriate environment
when longer-term care is required.

D. Place all children in a stable environment to which they can adjust,
where they will not become neglected again, and where they will not
become delinquent.

E. Operate the system efficiently so as to minimize the costs of achieving
all of the preceding objectives, or to achieve these objectives for the
largest number of children when resources are constrained.

Measurement Criteria

Objective A

1. Number of N-D petitions filed.

2. Number of different children named on N-D petitions.

3. Number of cases screened where a petition was not filed.

Objective B

1. Number and percent of children kept in their own home until Juvenile
Court hearing, after which they remain in their home.

Exhibit 10. (continued)

2. Number and percent of children avoiding institutionalization because of emergency caretakers.

3. Number and percent of children avoiding institutionalization because of placement in emergency foster homes.

4. Number and percent of children avoiding institutionalization because of homemakers.

Objective C

1. Number and percent of dispositions by the Juvenile Court that are considered to be good, questionable or bad as determined by professional opinion.

Objective D

1. Number and percent of children whose adjustment in placement is judged to be: satisfactory; questionable; unsatisfactory.

2. Number and percent of children moved from one placement to another.

3. Number and percent of children who develop delinquency records.

Objective E

1. Total cost of system.

2. Cost per child for each type of treatment.

Note: See Appendix A-1 for a summary of the program analysis in which these were considered.

Source: Adapted from Marvin R. Burt and Louis H. Blair, *Options for Improving the Care of Neglected and Dependent Children* (Washington, D.C.: The Urban Institute, March 1971).

Exhibit 11.   ILLUSTRATION OF OBJECTIVES AND
EVALUATION CRITERIA: FORT WORTH
TAKE-HOME PATROL CAR PROGRAM
ANALYSIS

Objectives

To reduce the amount of crime, particularly street crime; to prevent automobile accidents and personal injuries and deaths resulting from them; to improve citizen feelings of security; to improve the public image of the police; to improve police morale; and to operate the plan as efficiently as possible to minimize the cost of achieving the preceding objectives.

Measurement Criteria

1. Number and rate of crimes of various types—especially those potentially deterrable by the presence of a police car in the vicinity, such as auto theft, robberies, and street accidents.
2. Crime clearance rates.
3. Number of traffic accidents, injuries, and fatalities.
4. Index of citizen feeling of security, such as percent of citizens feeling safe walking in the streets at night.
5. Index of police-community relations, such as citizen ratings of police responsiveness, fairness, and courtesy.
6. Index of police morale, based on survey.
7. Program costs.

Note: See Appendix A-2 for a summary of the program analysis in which these were considered.

Source: Adapted from Donald M. Fisk, *The Indianapolis Police Fleet Plan* (Washington, D.C.: The Urban Institute, October 1970).

- Each program will probably have some impact on other groups that are *not* intended beneficiaries but are nonetheless affected beneficially or detrimentally by the program.

- The citizens of a community or state considered as a whole often comprise a category that should be explicity identified.

- In some cases, *future* clients (such as those who will become eligible, who will move into the city or state, or perhaps be born there) may be important groups to consider explicitly if their interests are likely to be affected by the program.

A list of characteristics for classifying typical client groups is presented in Exhibit 12. In addition to these general categories, each program is likely to be directed toward some unique client group or groups. Examples of groups that are likely to be affected by specialized programs are presented in Exhibit 13.

The analysts should try to estimate the impact of a program on different client groups according to each of the evaluation criteria—at least those criteria for which the impact seems likely to differ significantly among client groups.

7. *Always include dollar costs as one criterion.* Program costs should be estimated for each alternative. Estimaing cost is discussed in Chapter 4.

Sources for Identifying Relevant Objectives, Criteria, and Client Groups

It is rare to find program objectives, criteria, and client groups neatly described and packaged. However, a variety of sources may provide important clues to them:

- Legislative statements, such as ordinances, laws or resolutions sometimes discuss objectives. These are more likely to be available for state and federally originated programs than for local ones.
- Statements made by legislators, citizen groups, or individual citizens at public hearings discussing the program may indicate objectives. These may have been reported in press accounts.
- Program personnel will often be aware of many intended or unintended impacts that need to be considered as well as of population groups that are likely to be affected.

Exhibit 12.   TYPICAL CLIENT GROUP CLASSIFICATION
CHARACTERISTICS

1. Residence location—grouped by neighborhood, service
   area, precinct, etc., for local governments or by county,
   region, planning district, etc., for states.*

2. Sex

3. Age groups, such as youth and the elderly

4. Family incqme

5. Racial and ethnic groups

6. Problem or handicap groups—for example, individuals
   with alcohol problems or physical disabilities

7. Education level

8. Homeownership and type of dwelling

9. Employment status

10. Family size

11. Users of particular facilities

---

*In addition to reflecting residential location directly, this
category may be a reasonable proxy for other socioeconomic characteristics.

Exhibit 13.   ILLUSTRATION OF CLIENT GROUP
              CHARACTERISTICS OF SPECIALIZED
              SERVICE PROGRAMS

Type of service	Client groups likely to be of special relevance for program analysis
Recreation	Individuals in different neighborhoods or regions Sex—males and females often have different recreation interests Age—the very young and elderly have special needs Individuals with handicaps Individuals without access to an automobile Low-income families Users of specific types of recreation (e.g., golf, tennis, or hiking)
Drug abuse treatment	Individuals with different lengths and types of addiction Different age, sex, income class, or racial groups Families of addicts or potential addicts Citizens as a whole, particularly as potential victims of drug-related crime
Transportation	Individuals in different neighborhoods or regions Individuals without access to an automobile (e.g., the very young, the elderly, housewives left without an automobile, or those who cannot afford or do not want to drive) Individuals with physical handicaps Low-income families Individuals with unusual working hours
Solid waste collection	Individuals in different neighborhoods Elderly and physically handicapped individuals who may require special collection services Single vs. multiple housing unit customers Residential vs. commercial customers Rural vs. urban customers

• Government executives sometimes express program objectives and intended beneficiaries in statements to the legislature, the press, and the public, and in internal executive communications.

• Concerns expressed by clients of the service, perhaps obtained by an examination of government complaint records or by interviews, may identify service qualities of importance to them.

• Program evaluations and analyses conducted by other governments (including the federal government), academic or research institutions, and professional associations, should have identified objectives, criteria, and client groups.

Exhibit 14 contains a set of questions that might be asked by program analysts to help identify objectives, evaluation criteria, and appropriate program clients.

Selecting the Final Set of Effectiveness Measures

Analysts who follow the previously discussed steps and use their own experience will probably develop an extensive list of measures of effectiveness. The complete list may have to be narrowed to a relevant and manageable number so that data collection is not overwhelming. Some criteria for selecting a final set are shown in Exhibit 15.

Search for Alternatives

Central to every useful program analysis is the development of an appropriate set of alternatives which might achieve the program objectives. The following sources can often help identify program alternatives:

1. The analysis may have been initiated by specific proposals by government officials. These officials may also identify alternatives they wish considered.

2. Program personnel often have specific ideas on alternatives as well as a thorough knowledge of what agencies in other governments are trying.

Exhibit 14. QUESTIONS TO HELP IDENTIFY
OBJECTIVES, EVALUATION CRITERIA,
AND CLIENT GROUPS

1. What are the purposes of the program? Why was it (or should it be) adopted?

2. What is to be changed by the program, in both the immediate future and the long run? How would the program manager know if the program was working or not working? What would be accepted as evidence of success?

3. Who are the targets of the program? Is the community as a whole likely to be affected either directly or indirectly? Who else might be affected by the program?

4. What are possible side effects, both immediate and long-run?

5. What would be the likely consequences if the new program were introduced or if an existing program were discontinued? What would be the reaction of citizens in the community? Who would complain? Why would they complain? Who would be glad? Why?

3. Individuals and groups outside the government, including citizens, community organizations, public interest associations, and the news media will often make proposals.

4. Approaches of other governments to the same problem should be explored. Ideas being tried by others can often be identified through professional meetings, journals, government professional interest groups, and word of mouth.

5. Different sizes of the same alternative, such as expansions or contractions of an existing program, often need to be considered.

6. Combinations of individual alternatives may be defined as new alternatives.

7. During the analysis, new variations or new ideas may be suggested to alleviate the apparent weaknesses of basic alternatives that are found. Modifications in an alternative may be made to hedge

Exhibit 15. CRITERIA FOR SELECTING FINAL SET OF MEASURES

Importance

Does the measure provide useful and important information on the program which justifies the difficulties in collecting, analyzing or presenting the data?

Validity

Does the measure address the aspect of concern? Can changes in the value of the measure be clearly interpreted as desirable or undesirable, and can the changes be directly attributed to the program?

Uniqueness

Does the information provided by the measure duplicate or overlap with information provided by another measure?

Accuracy

Are the likely data sources sufficiently reliable or are there biases, exaggerations, omissions, or errors which are likely to make the measure inaccurate or misleading?

Timeliness

Can the date be collected *and analyzed* in time for the decision?

Privacy and Confidentiality

Are there concerns for privacy or confidentiality which would prevent analysts from obtaining the required information?

Costs of Data Collection

Can the resource or cost requirements for data collection be met?

Completeness

Does the final set of measures cover the major aspects of concern?

against these weaknesses. For example, if construction of a *new* facility seems risky, an alternative might be renting facilities until key uncertainties have been reduced or eliminated. Or, a program may be adopted on a trial basis; the decision on whether to adopt the full-scale program can be made when better information is obtained.

8. It might be useful to hold "brainstorming" sessions where analysis and agency personnel and perhaps others try to generate ideas. The purpose of such sessions would be to encourage imaginative, innovative, even radically new options.

An old story, and one we cannot vouch for, concerns a fish processing plant. It brought in live fish and kept them that way until needed. To reduce costs it wanted to reduce storage space but found that when the fish were packed tightly, they became inactive and the food flavor suffered. Many shapes and sizes of tanks were tried to get active movement of the fish without requiring large amounts of storage capacity. The alternative finally hit upon was to put a small sand shark in the tank. It worked wonders. It kept the fish quite active in a small area with only a small loss in fish.

9. Hard, knowledgeable, and careful thinking about a problem is often a neglected source of worthwhile alternatives.

For any given set of objectives there are likely to be a large number of conceivable alternatives (or variations) proposed. As a practical matter it is necessary to restrict the number of alternatives to be analyzed in detail. Most analyses consider no more than five or six alternatives. An analyst will have to make some early judgments, perhaps supported with preliminary, informal analysis and guidance from decision makers, to reduce a large list to a reasonable size. One study suggests four stages for screening: initial generation, cursory selection, intermediate selection, and final selection. [2]

Sometimes the program finally selected by government officials for implementation will *not* be among the alternatives explicitly examined in the analysis but a variation of one or more of them. This may be a result of political compromise, or because the analysis itself suggests that a new variation be generated, or it may occur because the initial alternatives are no longer appropriate.

---

[2]See Selma Mushkin and Brian Herman, "The Search for Alternatives: Program Options in a PPB System," The George Washington University, State-Local Finances Project (Washington, D.C., October 1968).

A caution: Decision makers sometimes have preconceived ideas about which alternative is preferable. Other alternatives might then be offered that are merely "sops" to analysis—impractical alternatives or minor variations of the preferred one. For meaningful analysis, however, only alternatives that are valid options, which actually address the problem under study and represent a range of possible actions, should be included.

The degree to which a set of alternatives includes departures from existing programs will significantly affect the task of estimating the alternatives' costs and effectiveness. To provide a preliminary basis for discussing the problems of, and approaches to, making estimates of costs and effectiveness, alternatives have been categorized into five types:

1. Present program extended at same level of effort;
2. Present program extended but at a different level of effort;
3. Other variations of the present program;
4. New programs with traditional concepts; and
5. New programs with new concepts.

A program analysis could study alternatives from a number of these categories. An emergency ambulance study proposed four alternatives of three different types:[3]

1. Maintain the status quo (Type 1);
2. Increase the number of ambulances at the district's hospital (Type 2);
3. Redistribute the existing ambulances in the district; locate some ambulances at satellite garages (Type 3); and
4. Increase and redistribute ambulances (a combination of Types 2 and 3).

While there is not always a clear distinction between these five types, we will briefly examine each, especially in terms of the problem involved in estimating costs and effectiveness.

---

[3]See Burt, *et al.,* op. cit.

1. *Present program extended at same level of effort.* The alternative most commonly considered in analyses is the existing program continued into the future with no significant change. This provides a baseline against which other alternatives can then be compared.

In this case, estimating costs is usually straightforward, at least for the near future. Many governments already project costs of current programs for at least one year as part of budget preparation; some state governments with biennial budgets make two-year projections. Where program cost projections do not exist, it is usually possible to estimate them without great difficulty. Still, quantitative estimates should be made of the effects of such factors as future inflation, pay raises, changes in workloads or caseloads, and replacement of equipment or facilities which might alter costs.

While cost of an existing program may be easy to assess, estimating its effectiveness is likely to be difficult. Few programs in state or local government have been the subject of recent program evaluation which might serve as an adequate basis for future projections of effectiveness. But with existing programs, at least crude assessments of past performance can often provide a basis for estimates of future performance. While estimates of future workload (caseload) or program demand are needed, they can often be based on past service experience.

Some external factors, however, may change a program's effectiveness in the future and should be considered. For example, the closing of local industrial plants may change the future effectiveness of existing manpower and welfare programs. In short, even the analysis of continuing and existing programs is likely to involve more than projecting current costs and effectiveness in a straight line on the basis of past experience.

For example, in the Fort Worth take-home police car analysis, the new proposal was compared to the existing police car arrangement. Costs for the existing arrangement were projected six years into the future, a fairly simple task since there were no planned increases in the size of the force, number of patrol officers, number of police cars, or time on patrol. But it was not so easy to estimate what future effectiveness would be. As in most other jurisdictions, crime and automobile accidents were increasing; however, the analysis simply assumed that these increases would continue at recent rates.[4]

---

[4]See Appendix A-2 and Fort Worth Research and Budget Department, "The Use of Police Patrol Cars by Off-Duty Patrolmen" (Fort Worth, Texas, 1970).

2. *Present program extended at a different level of effort.* An option commonly examined is the continuation of the same program concept but with a higher or lower level of resources. Some examples would be proposed increases in the number of motorized patrol units, reductions in the number of institutional facilities, and increases in the number of recreation facilities. Though straightforward, such actions affect both program cost and effectiveness.

Problems of estimation common to the alternative of continuing the existing program apply equally to this one. There are additional problems with this second alternative of estimating the costs and effects of revised program *size.* How much does it cost to add fifteen more police officers, or keep playgrounds open two additional hours per day, or train fifty additional persons? Usually, these questions cannot be answered reliably simply by using past average costs. Additional issues must be addressed: Are more facilities, equipment, or supervisory personnel also needed, and of what type? With respect to future needs for facilities or equipment, what unused capacity currently exists, and how much money can be saved by using this capacity? If a program alternative calls for a cutback, an analyst must be realistic and face up to the perennial stickiness in cutting back resources—considering persons with vested interests within and outside the government who may effectively resist cutbacks.

Similar problems exist in estimating effectiveness. An alternative which calls for another recreational facility or a new fire station will have an impact on effectiveness, but probably at a diminishing rate compared to previous additions. There may also be unevenness or "nonlinearity" in changes in effectiveness. For example, adding a few police may have virtually no impact on effectiveness, while drastically increasing the number in an area may lead to a substantial impact.

3. *Variations in present program procedures.* This type of alternative involves a modification in the design of the existing program, not simply a change in its level of operations. For example, police might revise their preventive patrol procedures; manpower agencies might modify their training programs; or the sanitation department might change from back-door to curbside pickup of garbage.

Costs and effectiveness for this type will be more difficult to estimate than for the previous types of alternatives, but estimates can continue to draw on experiences with the current program.

4. *New programs with traditional concepts.* Changes in current practices eventually become so great that they no longer represent mere variations of an existing program.

For example, a county's analysis of water recreational opportunities for children of low-income families considered three alternatives: (1) build six small community-size pools, (2) build three Olympic-size pools, and (3) bus children to a local beach. Neither of the latter two alternatives had been previously used by the government, but each was based on well-known elements. They could be considered alternatives of this type.[5]

This type of alternative formulation is one relatively safe way for governments to innovate. While the risks are larger than those of merely varying an existing program, they are not likely to be major. Since the proposed basic concepts often have already been tried somewhere, estimates of their costs and effectiveness can be based, at least in part, on past experiences of other governments.

5. *New programs with new concepts.* This is the least common type of alternative. It presents the greatest difficulties in estimating costs and effects. The risks for a government prevent its frequent use. However, options of this type may be the best way to make major progress over the long run, either in reducing costs or in increasing effectiveness. New drugs for treating some forms of mental illness and radical new approaches to rehabilitating inmates or alcoholics would fall into this category. New concepts are often tied to new technology, but they need not be.

The costs and effects of new programs with new concepts are particularly difficult to estimate, simply because they are "new" and thus largely untested. Whether a concept will really work at all may be unknown. Most new concepts take a long time to implement, refine, and test. By the time they are perfected, conditions may be quite different from those today. As will be noted in Chapters 4 and 5, techniques used to estimate the costs and effects of new concepts may be quite different from those used to estimate more familiar program alternatives. The problems with new concepts are vividly portrayed by attempts to introduce computer controlled traffic signals in several U.S. cities. Costs have been greatly underestimated, and

---

[5]See Burt, *et al.,* op. cit.

where the automated signals are working, it is not obvious that the intended effects are being achieved.[6] Small pilot tests of such alternatives often may be appropriate as a way of obtaining better cost and effectiveness information before committing resources on full-scale programs.

---

[6]See Harry P. Hatry et al., *Practical Program Evaluation for State and Local Government Officials* (Washington, D.C.: The Urban Institute, September 1972).

Chapter 4
Estimating Program Costs

After the steps described in the previous chapter have been taken, the question becomes how much each alternative will cost. The costs and effects of each alternative should be estimated for at least one year, preferably for several years, into the future.

The type of analysis discussed here is not the same as the more common budget and cost control type of costing. The emphasis here is on estimating future program costs for a number of alternatives, not on determining what has been spent and how efficiently. Nevertheless, current cost accounting systems will be an important source of information for program cost analysis. Cost estimation for program analyses is likely to place additional demands on, rather than become a substitute for, information currently obtained by internal management cost information systems.

This chapter presents some of the major issues in estimating costs.[1] They are discussed in terms of three phases of cost estimation: (1) describing the alternatives in sufficient detail so that each can be costed, (2) determining which costs should be included in the analysis, and (3) estimating the costs.

---

[1]For more detail see: The George Washington University, State-Local Finances Project, "The Role and Nature of Cost Analysis in a PPB System," PPB Note 6 (Washington, D.C., June 1968); Gene H. Fisher, *Cost Considerations in Systems Analysis* (Santa Monica, California: The RAND Corporation, December 1970); and J.D. McCullough, "Cost Analysis for Planning-Programming-Budgeting and Cost-Benefit Studies," RAND Publication P-3479 (Santa Monica, California: The RAND Corporation, November 1966).

Describing the Alternatives in Sufficient Detail so that Each Can Be Costed

Once the analyst has identified the alternatives to be considered in an analysis, the job is to describe each one in specific, operational terms so that estimates of cost can be made. The description should include major physical features: estimated number and type of personnel, supplies, equipment, facilities, etc. The description should also include aspects of the way the program will operate that may have a significant effect on costs and effectiveness.

How much detail is necessary to estimate costs? It is difficult to generalize. An example may help. The cost analysis of a new police helicopter program would need to develop such varied information as:

1. How often the helicopters would be used, including number of flying hours per year and for which time periods they would be needed.

2. Various characteristics of the helicopters and the plan of operation for estimating the fuel, maintenance, and facility costs.

3. Various characteristics of the plan of operation for estimating the number and types of personnel and their skill levels.

4. Support requirements, such as facilities and training programs.

A basic early step is to estimate how much demand there will be for the service and how many units of the various resources—such as the numbers of personnel, vehicles, and square feet of floor space—will be required to provide the service at that level. Exhibit 16 illustrates such calculations for estimating the number of patrol cars needed for two alternatives of the Fort Worth take-home patrol car analysis.

The program characteristics used to estimate costs should be compatible with the characteristics used to estimate effectiveness. This may seem obvious, but it is surprisingly easy to err here, especially if the program characteristics are changed frequently during the analysis. Many an analysis goes awry because it describes a special performance capability for a program alternative without counting in the added cost needed to achieve that extra capability.

Exhibit 16. ILLUSTRATION OF CALCULATIONS FOR
ESTIMATING RESOURCE INPUTS: NUMBERS
OF PATROL CARS NEEDED

	Alternative 1: all 289 eligible patrol officers take a car*	Alternative 2: 90% of all eligible patrol officers take a car*
Number of officers who refuse cars	0	29
Number of cars driven off duty	289	260
Extra backup cars (10%)	29	26
Total number of cars needed to support plan	318	286
Cars needed for nonpatricipants in plan	0	10
Total number of patrol cars needed	318	296
Less vacation car equivalents	11	10
Total cars needed	307	286
Current cars available	102	102
Additional cars needed	205	184

*Willingness to accept a car was considered by the analysts to be an important unknown. They tested two alternative assumptions, with costs subsequently estimated for each.

Source: Fort Worth Research and Budget Department, "The Use of Police Patrol Cars by Off-Duty Patrolmen" (Fort Worth, Texas, 1970).

In the previous example, if police helicopters are to operate at night, this will influence estimates of both cost and effectiveness. Details of night capabilities will need to be identified, such as the capability to track suspects. Cost estimates should include the added helicopter and ground equipment such as lights, as well as additional personnel and possible differential pay rates required to operate at night.

In general the analysts will need to work closely with agency personnel to make sure that all of the significant cost elements and operational factors, such as training, personnel, and facility availability, are included in the analysis.

Determining What Costs Should Be Included

For the most part, program analysis will involve consideration of alternatives to existing programs. The basic problem of cost analysis is to determine the *differences* in costs among alternatives. However, the government will also need to consider the *total* costs in relation to other government activities and of course to determine overall revenue requirements. The following concepts are usually involved:

1. *The cost analysis should focus on those cost elements that are likely to be substantial and that seem likely to vary significantly among the alternatives being considered.* Some cost elements will not vary significantly among the alternatives considered. For example, if all the alternatives require the same facilities and impose the same burden on existing facilities, then facility and maintenance costs would be the same and the analysis would not have to focus on them.

2. *For each alternative, analysts should determine which costs are fixed and which are variable.* For example, if a government is considering switching from one type of solid waste disposal operation to another, it is necessary to identify which of the vehicles and facilities already available can be used in the revised operation. Other costs, such as certain supervisory and facility costs, might not be affected or might be only partially affected by the change. Only those elements of cost that need to be increased or which can be decreased in the switchover from one system to the other are "variable."

In the long run no cost is actually fixed. For example, even the cost of departmental supervision is likely to increase as more and more programs are added to the department. Such increases might take the form of added staff, added facilities, or larger salaries and benefits for supervisory personnel in recognition of their increased responsibilities.

3. *The "marginal," "incremental," or "additional" costs incurred for a specific alternative are the relevant costs, not the average costs.* For example, suppose a government must decide whether to add one more swimming pool at a recreation facility or two more pools. The marginal cost of the second is how much more money it costs to build two pools than it costs to build one. Quantity discounts, for example, might reduce the unit cost of the second pool. If one pool could be obtained for $100,000 and two for $150,000, the relevant cost of the second is $50,000, not $75,000 (the average cost of the two).

4. *"Sunk" costs, those costs which have already been spent, are irrelevant.* For example, the fact that last year the government spent $500,000 to rehabilitate a facility is not relevant to the cost analysis.[2] There may be political reasons why the government will be concerned about the previous expenditures; the analyst concerned about the feasibility of implementing an alternative needs to be aware of these reasons. Nevertheless, recommending an inferior alternative because of the past $500,000 expenditure is merely throwing good money after bad. Only the future costs of the facility, such as those for operation, maintenance, and rehabilitation, are pertinent.

5. *Costs should be considered regardless of where they are carried on the accounting books, what organizational unit they are connected with, or where the money comes from.* Exhibit 17 presents a checklist of cost elements that might apply to any type of government program. Exhibit 18 illustrates cost elements for a specific analysis.

Costs are frequently borne by more than one department, funding source, or account. A common example is that of vehicle maintenance, which is performed in a centralized garage. For

---

[2]However, if there is a potential "salvage" value, e.g., for facilities, this return would be pertinent to any program alternative which includes disposal of the items.

Exhibit 17. ILLUSTRATIVE LIST OF ELEMENTS OF
PROGRAM COST: A GENERAL CHECKLIST

I.   *Investment costs*—costs which vary primarily with the size of
program but not its duration.

Initial planning, development, and engineering costs.
Test and evaluation
Land
Buildings and facilities
Equipment and vehicles
Initial training

II. *Recurring costs*—("operating and maintenance" costs)—costs
which vary with size and duration. These are typically estimated on a per-year basis.

Personnel salaries and wages
Fringe benefits
Maintenance and repair of equipment, vehicles, and build-
ings
Direct contributions and payments to citizens, e.g., welfare
payments to the needy
Payments to nongovernmental institutions for services for
citizens, e.g., payments to agencies for foster home ser-
vices
Miscellaneous materials and supplies
Miscellaneous support (overhead) costs
Refresher training, and recruitment and training costs of
replacement employees

Source: The George Washington University, State-Local
Finances Project, "The Role and Nature of Cost
Analysis in a PPB System," (Washington, D.C., June
1968).

Exhibit 18.   ILLUSTRATIVE COST ELEMENT LIST FOR A
POLICE HELICOPTER PROGRAM ANALYSIS

Investment costs

Planning and tests
Helicopters
Initial purchase of spare parts
Purchasing of land for maintenance, storage and landing
Construction of helicopter pads, fueling, communications,
    and other operating facilities
Initial training of crews
Initial training of maintenance personnel

Recurring costs

Pay and fringe benefits of crews
Pay and fringe benefits of maintenance and other support
    personnel
Fuel and oil
Maintenance parts
Crew training—replacement crews or refresher training
Repair and maintenance of facilities
Insurance—liability and damage to helicopter and personnel
Replacement of helicopters and other major equipment

program analysis purposes the costs for this maintenance should be
included in the costs of the programs that use the vehicles. Building
maintenance is a similar example—police programs should be
charged with relevant maintenance costs for facilities.

Another case is employee benefits. These benefits, which may
add 15 to 30 percent or more to personnel costs, are typically charged
to a separate account. Capital costs, even though handled in other
funds and in a separate budget document, also need to be included in
program analyses.

The analyst should consider the future cost implications of each
of the alternatives. A decision to build a facility or buy a large item of
equipment in one budget year imposes future operating and
maintenance costs. A federal grant that covers only certain

investments such as construction costs will often entail future expenditures for maintenance. The cost analysis needs to include these obligations.

6. *Some program alternatives will generate revenues, such as bridge and highway tolls, charges to consumers for water and sewers or health service, and recreation user fees.* Such revenues as grants from the federal government may also be associated with particular program alternatives. The amount of these revenues, when believed to be substantial, needs to be estimated. *Relevant revenues should probably be considered either as offsets to total costs or as "side benefits."* In general, where the receipts are specifically collected in the course of program operation (such as with tolls, golf course fees, and water and sewer charges), these revenue items may be considered as offsets to total costs. The choice of whether associated revenues should be treated as a cost offset or a side benefit should not significantly affect the program decision, since in either case the revenues will have been explicity considered.

The summary tables in the program analysis report should probably display three lines for each program alternative: total costs, offsetting revenues, and the net cost to the government.

7. *Some alternatives may affect the costs of other program areas.* A slum clearance program might result in future reductions in the need for fire and crime protection services for the cleared area; on the other hand, it might also lead to increased demand for park and recreation services. [3] These can be important considerations, especially for analyses considering large-scale changes. Estimating such effects is often complex and particularly difficult.

8. *If resources are put into one program, opportunities to use the same resources elsewhere have been foregone.* The value of these foregone opportunities is the "opportunity cost" of putting resources into the selected program. This "value" is, therefore, relevant to program selection.

---

[3]Some financial repercussions of a program might also occur *outside* the government. For example, changes to transportation systems or in housing may have considerable effects on many types of businesses in the area—some favorable, some unfavorable. Or the gain in future earnings to individual citizens due to improved education or employment programs also may mean increased tax revenue. However, those outside-the-government cost effects should be distinguished from the inside-the-government costs and probably are better considered as economic impacts to be included in effectiveness estimation than as part of program cost analysis.

In program analysis, the explicit identification and assessment of alternatives is a practical way to take account of opportunity costs. To illustrate, a government might use land it already owns for a new public facility. It would not incur any additional land costs, but would be giving up the opportunity to use the land for other purposes. The alternative use of the land is an important consideration. The analysis might attempt to impute a dollar value to this land (perhaps using current market value) and include this imputed value as a cost. Or it might avoid this imputation and instead consider other land uses as explicit alternatives to be evaluated. If imputed values are used, since they are not actual dollar outlays, they should be separately identified so as not to distort the estimation of funding outlays actually needed for an alternative. However, if one option was, for example, to sell government land, then the resulting revenues (perhaps including any taxes generated by the land or improvements to it) would be an important alternative opportunity.

Where land or facilities have other meaningful uses, the analysis should at least explicitly indicate as a "negative benefit" or undesirable effect the loss of the land for these other future uses.

Estimating the Costs

Five approaches or sources for estimating costs follow:

1. Unadjusted current data applied to the future;
2. "Vendor" estimates;
3. Internal "engineering" estimates;
4. Statistical estimation, and
5. Cost factors and cost models.

For any given analysis some or all of these approaches might be used. Each of these is discussed briefly:

1. *Unadjusted current data applied to the future.* This costing approach is primarily applicable to costs that are not expected to change significantly. As an example, the latest salary and employee benefit scales might simply be used to estimate future personnel costs, or current data on the number of personnel or staff-hours required to perform a specific task might be used to estimate the future requirements for that task, if the task appears stable.

There are severe limitations on this approach, particularly if demand for the service changes or if technological improvements in equipment are anticipated. If, for example, a government's emergency rescue vehicles are expected to become more complex in the future (e.g., more automatic monitoring or telecommunications devices and emergency equipment), higher costs per vehicle might be anticipated. There also might be higher maintenance costs, and additional training costs for operation. In this case, it would not be appropriate to use the unadjusted current data.

Price level changes may, of course, also affect the future costs of program components even if nothing else changes. This problem is discussed later.

2. *"Vendor" estimates.* Certain programs may involve pieces of equipment or facilities for which price quotations can be obtained from a seller or builder. If the quotes are for already existing items or such items with minor modifications, the prices should be accurate. However, a firm commitment is not always implied in the estimate, and complications might arise in making the item.

3. *Internal "engineering" estimates.* As new programs are proposed, involving components significantly different from current or past program components, other techniques are needed. The major technique currently in use is for technical experts—government employees or consultants—to prepare cost estimates for the new components. For example, city or state engineers or others doing the program design may also estimate the cost.

One difficulty in engineering estimates is that if many program alternatives and variations are examined, the time required for the estimates may be substantial.

4. *Statistical estimation.* This method is less commonly used in most state and local governments.

Predicting future costs, especially for programs with new and perhaps unusual characteristics, is a very difficult task. Expert judgment should be helpful and will be necessary, but the cost analysis often can be aided considerably by the use of statistical techniques. Statistics can help extract useful information from data on past performance and help make inferences as to future costs or performance.

The use of statistics can be very simple or very complicated. The simpler techniques of statistics are familiar. For example, to derive a figure for the fuel and maintenance cost of police cars used in a traffic control program, the previous year's costs for all traffic control police cars can be divided by the number of cars to obtain an average cost per car. Assuming no price increases or significant changes in the nature of the police cars to be used, the average cost per car could then be used to estimate the cost of proposed alternative programs involving any number of police cars of the same type.

A more advanced technique is *regression analysis.* In the example shown in Exhibit 19, the analysts used a "simple" regression analysis to estimate the future maintenance costs of police patrol cars. The analysts assumed that the major explanatory variable in the cost equation was the number of miles driven. The diagram show a hypothetical "scatter diagram" on which are plotted the most recent year's data on the existing patrol cars. From the appearance of the scatter diagram, the analysts estimate that a straight line would fit the data. Using standard mathematical procedures (with some computer assistance) a line of "best fit" can be derived and is shown on the scatter diagram. The equation for the line is also shown. The resulting equation can then be used to help estimate future maintenance costs of police patrol cars of a similar type to those in the sample.

In many analyses, considerably more complicated assumptions may be necessary, requiring more complex statistical techniques and more complex equations. With more than one explanatory variable, "multiple" regression analysis rather than "simple" regression analysis is required.

To use such equations for estimating future program costs, it is first necessary to estimate the values for each of the explanatory variables, e.g., the "annual mileage per vehicle" in Exhibit 19. This itself may often be difficult.

5. *Cost factors and cost models.* There may be a need in a particular program analysis for the examination of numerous program alternatives. For some government services, fairly frequent program analyses may be needed. Thus, there may develop a repetitive need for the preparation of cost factors and cost equations which can be applied to many different costing problems. Statistical equations such as those already illustrated as well as simple cost factors—such as the annual maintenance cost per unit—might be appropriate for each major program area. These would be updated periodically for use as costing problems arose.

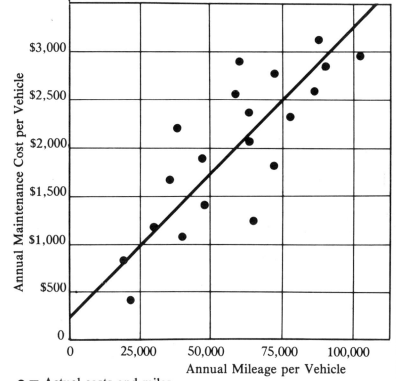

Exhibit 19.   AN EXAMPLE OF REGRESSION ANALYSIS:
ESTIMATED ANNUAL MAINTENANCE COSTS
PER VEHICLE

Estimated Cost = $250 + $.03 x miles driven
(If a vehicle were to be driven 75,000 miles
next year, the estimated maintenance costs
would be $2,500.)

● = Actual costs and miles
driven by an individual vehicle in
the last year.

Source: The George Washington University State-Local Finances
Project, "The Role and Nature of Cost Analysis in a PPB
System," (Washington, D.C., June 1968).

Individual cost factors or cost equations might be prepared at any convenient level of aggregation. For example, some might cover a single accounting object class, others might cover a subdivision of an object class, and still others an aggregation of object classes. This will depend upon the particular circumstances such as the nature of the available data and the use to which the factors and equations will be put.

These cost factors and cost equations together could provide estimates of the total program cost for different variations of a certain type of program. This can be called a "cost model." Such cost models might be constructed for different types of programs. If the cost model involves much computation and is used frequently enough, computerization might be appropriate.

Some Special Problems in Cost Analysis

Four special problems need to be mentioned:

1. First is the issue of price changes. Should adjustments be made to reflect possible future price changes in the various elements of cost? This problem is particularly important if some of the alternatives are likely to be more affected by future price increases than others. Estimating future changes in general price levels is difficult. In addition to the problem of attempting to predict the trend of the economy, the price index is likely to differ for each element of cost. That is, the cost of payroll, of construction, and of various types of equipment each potentially requires its own price index. One concern is that the price level estimates could be self-fulfilling—that contractors, unions, or other claimant groups would become aware of the estimates and would be unlikely to settle for less than the estimated increases.

Perhaps such projections should be made only when it appears clear that the program choice could be significantly affected by price changes.

2. A second special problem in program cost analysis is the need to provide some indication of the magnitude of uncertainty of the cost estimates. Estimates of costs and effectiveness will seldom be precise, especially for years beyond the next budget year. Estimates for unfamiliar alternatives to within 10 to 25 percent will often be as accurate as can be expected. The magnitude and likelihoods of cost uncertainties may affect final program decisions and should, if

significant, be assessed as well as possible. Techniques can range from simply labeling estimates as "reasonably accurate" or "highly uncertain" to more elaborate techniques which attempt to estimate quantitatively the likelihood and size of the uncertainty. Handling uncertainty is discussed further in Chapter 6.

3. The third special problem in cost analysis is how to summarize future costs for each program alternative. Four options are:

a. Present the cost for each year;
b. Summarize all costs for a given number of years;
c. Calculate the "present worth" or "present value" of the expected outlays; and
d. A combination of the above.

The "present-worth" technique requires the government to select a specific rate of return (i.e., an "interest" or "discount" rate). Then analysts compute the present worth of the expenditures for each future year for each program alternative. For example, an alternative might require the expenditure of $1 million now, $1 million a year from now, and $1 million two years from now. Assuming an annual discount rate of 10 percent, approximately $2.74 million invested today at 10 percent interest would provide just enough to meet the three $1 million payments. Other expenditure patterns could similarly be translated into present worths. A second program requiring expenditures of $0.2 million now and $1.4 million in each of the next two years is equivalent to about $2.63 million now at a rate of 10 percent. Therefore, other things being equal, the second program is more desirable because its present worth is less, even though both programs require the same outlays of funds.

A major problem in using the present-worth technique is the selection of the appropriate interest rate. This selection is difficult and controversial.

In most individual program analyses, the consideration of the present worth of future flow of costs will not alter the choice of programs and therefore may not be worth the effort. The present-worth technique should be used primarily when alternatives with similar total costs but considerably different time phasing of expenditures are under examination.

4. Finally, there is a tendency in cost analysis to attempt to be overly precise in situations which do not warrant it. This can be both wasteful of effort and misleading. Analysts should roughly estimate the magnitude of the costs involved and how much precision is necessary, then adjust cost analyses to those dimensions.

Chapter 5
Estimating Effectiveness

It is difficult to estimate how effective an existing program will be in the future. It is even more challenging to predict the consequences of new or modified programs. But estimates, even crude, are necessary.

The basic problems are the future uncertainties under which a proposed program will have to operate and the likelihood of success under those conditions. The further one projects a program into the future, the more uncertain one's projections become; even a one-year projection can entail considerable uncertainty.

The more that is known about a program alternative and the conditions in which it will operate, the easier and more accurate the projection will be. Inevitably, estimating the effectiveness of a program requires many assumptions about the relation between government resources (including the ways these resources are combined and put to use) and outcomes. This is a large part of the art of program analysis.

It is difficult to describe the many approaches that can be used to estimate future program effectiveness and the innumerable situations and variations program analysts can expect to face. However, an attempt is necessary, and nine general approaches are identified below. These approaches are somewhat similar to those described for estimating program costs. We distinguish between approaches for estimating the effectiveness of those programs that are extensions or minor variations of a government's existing programs, and those used for programs that are new. These approaches are summarized in Exhibit 20. [1]

---

[1] An approach to estimating effectiveness that is often used—but which we feel is rarely appropriate—is to assume that effectiveness is proportional to the amount of inputs, or resources, applied. One can, for example, assume that adding 10 percent to the amount of resources applied to a service will improve the quality of the service by 10 percent. This approach has the advantage of simplicity, but, of course, it begs the question of whether more resources will help and, for given combinations of resources, how effectively.

Exhibit 20. APPROACHES FOR ESTIMATING
EFFECTIVENESS

*Approaches for Extensions or Minor Variations of Existing
Programs*

1. Use past performance as the estimate of future
   effectiveness.
2. Adjust past performance by estimates of future conditions affecting effectiveness.

Approaches for Alternatives New to the Jurisdiction

3. Use past performance in another government as the
   estimate for future effectiveness.
4. Obtain performance estimates from vendor.
5. Develop "engineered" estimates.
6. Employ mathematical modeling techniques.
7. Use "expert" judgment.
8. Use a "simulated adversary" process.
9. Use information from a limited trial of the program.

Estimating Effectiveness for Alternatives that Are Extensions or Minor Variations of Existing Programs

1. Data on the performance of past programs can be used as an estimate of future performance. Unfortunately, information on existing programs is frequently lacking and a special program evaluation is likely to be needed. In addition, the use of such past performance information assumes that conditions will not change substantially in the future. For example, if the criminal apprehension rate for the past year is 20 percent, this figure can be used as an estimate for the future of continuing the same program. This approach is certainly simple, but it is probably overused. The assumption of stability is questionable in many, if not most, cases.

2. Past performance data can be adjusted by estimating likely effects of changes in future conditions on performance. There are many ways to do this. One way entails the use of time series data: Rather than using only performance data for the past year, an analyst takes an average of several past years' performance data or uses the data of several years to compute a projection line based on recent trends. For example, if the apprehension rate for the past year is 20 percent, and if in prior years the rate had been gradually increasing, a higher apprehension rate would be used in projections. The assumption is that the trend over a number of years is a more reliable indicator of the future than a single year's data.

Time alone should not be considered an adequate explainer of future conditions in most situations. Changes in the overall population, in the client mix (such as age, sex, income, race, and residential location), and in physical characteristics of the jurisdiction (such as new housing and transportation) may affect the performance of program alternatives. While the effects can become quite complex, the analyst can often identify certain key conditions that are changing. Once these changes are identified, their effects can be projected into the future and used to modify estimates of the program's effectiveness. For example, an examination of solid waste landfill disposal alternatives would require, in part, projections of changes in the numbers of households and of waste generated per household. This would yield an estimate of future demand for solid waste disposal by residential units; this estimate could then be added to estimates of waste from other sources and be compared with present disposal capacity and the capacity of other landfill options to determine how effective each is in handling projected future needs.

Estimating Effectiveness for Alternatives that Are New to the Government

3. *If a proposed alternative has been tried by another government, useful data from that government's experience may be available.* Unfortunately, such data are likely to be inadequate, since governments seldom make explicit provision for evaluative information. Also, analysts should be cautious when using published reports, since they may be mainly public relations documents or may not have been based on systematic program evaluation.

For example, a recent examination of a computerized system for allocating police resources by geographic area and time of day indicated that, despite the apparent belief that response times had been reduced, actual response time data had not been collected and could not have been analyzed to support that belief..[2]

Analysts may need to make onsite visits to obtain detailed program descriptions and performance data. This was a key step, for example, in the Fort Worth program analysis of the Indianapolis police take-home car plan. [3]

The plan was introduced in September 1969. Prompted by an expression of interest by the Fort Worth City Council, the city of Fort Worth, with the assistance of the Indianapolis Police Department and The Urban Institute, in the spring of 1970 undertook a systematic evaluation of the costs and effects of the program experience to date. That report was used in estimating costs and effects of a similar plan for Fort Worth.

Performance reports prepared shortly after the initiation of a program should be considered with caution. A program generally requires six to twelve months, and often longer, before its operation stabilizes and negative or unintended effects can be detected.

Even if good evaluative information from other jurisdictions is available, it does not remove the need for an independent analysis of the program. The attractiveness of any alternative depends in part on the conditions of the particular state or local jurisdiction. For example, before making a decision on a police take-home car plan, a city should consider how many of its reported crimes could be prevented by use of marked police cars.

4. *In some circumstances, vendors can provide performance estimates for equipment-oriented alternatives, or at least performance information on the equipment itself.* Vendor estimates, of course, can be expected to be optimistic; they are also likely to be limited to the immediate intended performance of the equipment and not to the variety of impacts—especially negative ones—that may occur when the equipment is used by fallible human beings in sometimes less than ideal working environments.

---

[2]For information on this and other experiences of the difficulty of obtaining evaluative information on innovations that have been tried, see Part IV of The Urban Institute and the International City Management Association, *The Challenge of Productivity Diversity* (Washington, D.C.: The National Commission on Productivity, June 1972).

[3]See Donald Fisk, *The Indianapolis Police Fleet Plan,* (Washington, D.C.: The Urban Institute, 1970).

5. *In some cases, the analyst has to synthesize an estimate from known facts about the alternative, or even use "engineered" estimates based on anticipated characteristics of the proposed system.* This is particularly so with alternatives that involve new technologies or new procedures for which appropriate comparison data are not available. For example, a new solid waste disposal system might be crudely assessed by using data from the design and the technical specifications to estimate the amount of waste that the system could handle on a daily basis and the amount of pollution that it would yield.

Analysts should also assess whether the estimated effectiveness is likely to remain the same or change significantly in the years following introduction. If significant changes seem likely, crude estimates of the amount of the change should be made. This type of analysis is filled with uncertainties, however, and new technologies rarely perform, at least at first, as well as anticipated.

6. *At times, various mathematical modeling techniques can be used.* Formal models are particularly useful (a) where there are many and complex interactions among the factors affecting program effectiveness, and (b) where historical performance data are available and can be used in quantitative form. [4]

Analyses of the number and location of emergency ambulances and fire stations have used such models to make response time calculations. In these cases a major element in the effectiveness calculations is to attempt to estimate the travel time from a fire station or ambulance location to the fire or client needing emergency care. Mathematical models are used to stimulate the geographical network in the jurisdiction. Analysts can thereby compute response times for varying numbers and locations of fire stations or ambulances, so as to select that configuration that minimizes response times. Considerable data on the existing street network and vehicle speeds are needed as input to the models. It would be desirable to consider likely future changes to the street network and the vehicles

---

[4]A survey of federally supported models, including a listing by subject area, is contained in Gary Fromm, William L. Hamilton and Diane E. Hamilton, *Federally Supported Mathematical Models*, NTIS-PB 241562 (Washington, D.C.: Data Resources, Inc. and ABT Associates, Inc., June 1974). The survey also provides model cost information.

to make the network and vehicle speeds more appropriate to expected future conditions.[5]

A variety of mathematical modeling techniques, some requiring computer assistance, has also been used to allocate police resources by time of day and day of week, to route garbage trucks, and to select toll booth arrangements. However, analysts can often use less complex and non-computer-based mathematical models. Separate analyses by two cities to allocate fireboats for protecting the water-front involved fairly simple mappings of the placement of fireboats relative to projected call locations and frequency. If the number of combinations examined had been greater, a computerized approach might have been more efficient.

Mathematical modeling might be used to directly estimate a service's effectiveness or to project intermediate factors affecting future demand for a service so that alterntives could be rated against them. A variety of statistical, operations research, and mathematical techniques are available that on occasion will be quite useful.

A word of caution on the use of models is necessary.[6] The critical assumptions built into models must be clearly articulated by the model builders and understood by the decision makers, since these assumptions usually influence the results significantly. Too often large models become so complex that only the computer knows what is going on. Model applications need to be reviewed beforehand to determine the probable amount of improvement over simpler approaches. Large-scale models requiring computer processing are expensive to develop and to "debug" for proper operation. The greatest payoffs from a large model are likely to occur where they are used often enough—or on extremely important and costly program decisions—to justify the initial development and programming costs.

7. *When none of the previous methods can be employed, expert judgment may be appropriate.* Experts may be government personnel

---

[5] For further discussions see: Mathias L. Spiegel, and E.S. Savas, *Emergency Ambulance Service for the City of New York* (New York: Office of the Mayor, March 8, 1968); Kenneth L. Kraemer, *A Systems Approach to Decision Making—Policy Analyses in Local Government* (Washington, D.C.: The International City Management Association, 1973); and Thomas R. Willemain, "The Status of Performance Measures for Emergency Medical Services" (Cambridge, Massachusetts: Operations Research Center, Massachusetts Institute of Technology, July 1974).

[6] Two criticisms of large-scale model efforts are contained in Douglas B. Lee, Jr., "Requiem for Large-Scale Models," *Journal of the American Institute of Planners,* May 1973; and Ida R. Hoos, *Systems Analysis in Public Policy—A Crituqe* (Berkeley, California: University of California Press, 1972).

or persons outside the particular government who have extensive experience in the program area. Their judgments can be used for making direct estimates of an alternative's effectiveness or for estimating the future values of various factors needed for effectiveness calculations. A systematic procedure for making judgments should be used, and the judgments should be documented and substantiated as well as possible. Such sophisticated approaches as Delphi,[7] which uses anonymous opinions of a number of experts to refine progressively a specific projection, can sometimes be helpful. But these sophisticated approaches tend to be time-consuming and relatively expensive; they are probably justifiable only if the program is very important to the government.

Experts could be used merely to *rank* the relative effectiveness of alternatives in terms of a particular characteristic, but quantitative *ratings* of effectiveness are preferable. For example, analysts might need to assess the degree to which various probation and parole service approaches would lead to a reduction in recidivism. At the very least, a number of experts might rank each proposed approach as "better," "worse," or "about the same" as the existing approach. More useful for the purposes of analysis (but more difficult for the expert) would be estimates of the degree of success.

8. *A "simulated adversary process" may sometimes be appropriate.* Under this approach, each major alternative is assigned to a different "team," and each team then builds as strong a case as possible for its assigned alternative, probably using some of the techniques already described. This approach is appropriate primarily when analysts are dealing with important issues that have differing impacts on different groups in the community. In such cases the approach can provide government officials with a broadened perspective of the pros and cons of the various alternatives.

9. *Finally, if sound estimates are not obtainable, and if government officials believe that a particular alternative has considerable*

---

[7]See, for example, H. Sackman, *Delphi Assessment: Expert Opinion, Forecasting, and Group Process*, RAND Publication R-1238-PR (Santa Monica, California: The RAND Corporation, April 1974).

*potential but that uncertainties are too great for a full-scale commit-
ment, the government might undertake a limited trial to provide more
reliable information on the new program.* This approach is most
appropriate in cases where a short-term program of limited scope is
feasible and where only small initial investments are needed for
manpower and capital additions. The trial approach has another
advantage when past experience is not available: a trial is likely to detect
unintended, perhaps negative, program effects.

One example of the trial approach is in crime control, where it is
extremely difficult to predict the effectiveness of various manpower
allocation or patrol strategies such as team policing. In such cases,
the government might undertake a one-year trial of a specific strategy
in particular neighborhoods to obtain information on the strategy's
effectiveness.

Many difficulties are associated with this approach, however. For
example, many programs may not be adequately evaluated on the
basis of a one-year experience. Start-up problems might temporarily
degrade performance, producing inaccurate indications of long-term
performance. On the other hand, special attention paid to the program
might result in better short-term performance, yielding misleading
indications of long-term performance.

If a government undertakes the trial approach, it should provide
for a systematic program evaluation.[8] The trial should be designed
realistically, and critical evaluation criteria should be identified in
advance. Trials are often conducted without adequate concern for the
need for performance data. As a result, the government is likely to
have very little information about program effectiveness by the end of
the trial period.[9]

Some Illustrations of Approaches

Due to the numerous variations of program alternatives and
problems in effectiveness estimation, generalizations about appropriate effectiveness estimation procedures are difficult to make. In

---

[8]A detailed discussion of program evaluation is contained in a companion volume,
Practical Program Evaluation for State and Local Governments (Washington, D.C.: The
Urban Institute, 1972).

[9]Note that, as discussed in Chapter 3 in the section on the search for alternatives,
the option of undertaking a limited trial of a new program is itself an alternative that
needs to be assessed as to its costs and effects—and compared with those of going ahead
with one of the alternatives without such a trial.

most instances, a combination of the techniques noted above will be appropriate. The following examples—and the more detailed presentations in Appendix A—illustrate typical problems and the ways that specific techniques might be applied to them.

1. Neglected and Dependent Children

In an analysis of ways to reduce the number of neglected and dependent children and particularly the number placed in a children's institution (described in more detail in Appendix A-1), estimates were sought of the effectiveness of increasing emergency homemaker service, increasing emergency foster homes, and providing initial screening of requests for neglected and dependent care. Each of the previous year's cases in which a child received neglected and dependent services was categorized as to the reason for the child coming into the system. A professional social worker examined these cases and made judgments as to which cases an emergency homemaker, an emergency foster home, or initial screening could have been used to keep children in their own home or in the home of someone who could provide appropriate care. The number and percent of cases in which a child could have avoided being institutionalized were then calculated.

The number of children entering the child care system and their reasons for entering were assumed to be the same in future years as in the most recent year for which data were available. If more time had been allowed, the analysts might have collected data from past years for a time trend analysis to project more accurately the number of children of the various types likely to enter the system in future years. Professional judgment could then have been used to estimate the number of children of each type who could avoid institutionalization through the additional services provided by each proposed option. A more extensive analysis might have examined the changing population makeup in the county (using statistical analysis) to project any significant changes in population characteristics and the likely effects of these population changes on the type and number of neglected-dependent children in the future (considering such factors as increasing or decreasing affluence in the county among parents with children under 18 years old.)

2. Ambulances, Fire Stations, and Patrol Cars

Analyses of the desired number and location of emergency

ambulances, fire stations, or police patrol cars have generally used response time as the measure of effectiveness. This measure however, does not take into account the value of reduced response time in saving lives, reducing fire damage, or apprehending criminals. This makes it difficult to determine whether the expense of added stations, ambulances, or patrol cars and the accompanying reduction in response time is worth the additional cost. Without such information, decisions will probably be based on relatively uninformed judgments.

To improve the information available for such decisions, experts might be used to estimate the impacts of various response time rates for particular client conditions. By examining past ambulance cases, analysts and medical experts would identify a series of representative scenarios. They might, for example, specify the type of problems causing the call for an ambulance, the patient's condition at the time of the call, and such critical patient characteristics as age. The medical experts would then estimate the likely effects of various delay times. In a more ambitious analysis, the effects of various delay times might be estimated more reliably by examining a large number of actual cases on which response time, patient data, and patient outcome information were available. Statistical analysis would then be used to help estimate the effects of various response times. The analysts and experts could estimate the probable frequency of each scenario from examining the frequency of past cases.

A time series analysis could be used to adjust past frequencies and project trends in the number of each type of case. The analysts would then be able to estimate the number of patients who would be helped by various reductions in response time as a result of changes in the number and stationing of ambulances.

3. Helicopters

To analyze the potential value of helicopters in apprehending crime suspects, a sample of past crime incidences might be examined to determine whether a helicopter might have been useful in each situation. Such conditions as weather, visibility, location, and circumstances of the crime would be included in the consideration. Expert judgment—perhaps by a police officer from a city which uses a helicopter—would be used to estimate the potential consequences of the use of the helicopter in each instance. The frequency of cases in which the helicopter would be helpful would be calculated from the statistical sample of incidents (after adjusting for possible factors that would affect the future frequency of each type of circumstance).

4. Parole and Probation Counselors

A difficult type of analysis problem—of a kind that frequently arises in social service programs—occurs in considering whether to increase the number of parole and probation counselors. Of particular concern is the effect, if any, of changes in the caseload per worker on client recidivism. The analysis might begin by making estimates of future caseloads (categorized by the type of offender), based on past caseload trends and recent policies of the courts and law enforcement agencies.

The analysis might then examine the past effectiveness of the current parole and probation officer staff in terms of both (1) the number and percent of cases in which probation or parole revocations occurred, and (2) the number and percent with criminal records *after* completing probation-parole (perhaps determined by follow-ups on a sample of former parolees or probationers).

Three approaches may be used for estimating the amount of improvement from reduced caseloads: (a) Undertake a carefully monitored trial to determine the effects of caseload reduction (preferably this would include "control" and "experimental" groups such as by randomly assigning probationers and parolees to counselors with varying caseloads). This approach will require many months before adequate impact data become available. (b) Examine a sample of past cases, to identify, by category of parolee, the amount of counseling that the counselor was able to provide, and the apparent counseling success for the various levels of effort applied. (c) Have professional "experts" examine past cases to estimate the degree to which the individual might have been helped if various amounts of additional time had been provided (a "scenario" approach).

5. Drug Abuse Treatment

In a drug abuse treatment program (and, in fact, for most government human resource treatment programs), it is important to classify clients as to the expected difficulty of rehabilitating them. Programs treating clients with severe drug problems and low levels of motivation would probably have lower rehabilitation rates than programs treating clients with less severe drug problems and higher levels of motivation. Rehabilitation rates should be estimated for each category of client difficulty. Estimates of the number of persons likely to fall into each category in the future are also required in order to estimate the number of persons rehabilitated by each alternative treatment program. Rehabilitation rates for the various client categories might be calculated by using past rehabilitation rates from existing programs or similar programs of other governments or by using expert judgment. Appendix A-3 describes in more detail effectiveness estimation for drug treatment programs.

6. Welfare Staffs

Suppose a state or county public welfare agency wants to assess a proposal to increase its inspection staff for checking the accuracy of welfare eligibility determinations and payment amounts and to correct errors. Analysts could review existing inspection results, or perhaps make a special investigation of a random sample of cases, to determine the percentage of cases investigated with inaccurate payments and the average dollar amount involved in each error. This percentage might be assumed to apply also to the future. It would then be necessary to estimate how many inequities would be uncovered by additional case inspections. For example, if the sampling of cases indicated inaccuracies in one out of ten cases, then about ten investigations would be required per error found. Estimates of the amount of time required per inspector could be based on past experience with various types of cases. The number and amount of incorrect payments and the resulting corrections could then be estimated for the number of investigators proposed.

7. Solid Waste Disposal

An analysis of future solid waste disposal alternatives might contain the following steps:

(a) Projections of the solid waste generated in the future would be estimated based on projections of the population and the amount of waste generated per capita (which itself might be changing) and on any projected increase in industrial growth. Such projections of future need might be made by various statistical means including time trend projection as well as more complicated approaches which utilize a number of other variables in addition to time.

(b) The treatment capacity for each type of refuse of each solid waste disposal alternative would be estimated based on the technical characteristics of each option. "Engineering" calculations might be needed for new technological alternatives being considered.

(c) The capabilities estimated in (b) can then be compared against the need estimated in (a) to indicate the ability of each alternative to meet the need. Because of the long lead time needed before certain of the alternatives could become operational (when an alternative requires the construction of new facilities) and because of the likely annual growth of the amount of solid waste, the ability of each alternative to meet the need for solid waste disposal should probably be considered for each future year of relevance to the analysis.

(d) The estimate of the pollution generated by each alternative would be based on the amount of waste disposed and the technical characteristics of each disposal alternative, probably based on "engineering" calculations. (Note: it would also be desirable to estimate the resulting ambient quality of the air or water and resulting hazard level. These involve added difficult steps that would preferably consider such factors as: the likely future of air or water quality from all other sources, weather conditions, and the interaction of the various pollutants.)

Final Comment on Effectiveness Measurement

The above examples merely touch the surface in illustrating the great variety of effectiveness estimation issues that are likely to arise even in a single state or local government. The approaches identified do not provide detailed how-to-do-it suggestions. But, at least, the approaches may suggest some ideas as to starting points for individual effectiveness estimation problems.

Chapter 6
Miscellaneous Analytical Considerations

Needs Assessment

A major aspect of program analysis is determining how well an alternative will meet the estimated need for a service. The term "need," however, is vague, implies a variety of meanings, and is difficult to express quantitatively.

In general, analysts must consider both *expressed* demand, based, for example, on the past usage of the particular service, and *latent* (hidden) demand. The latter is the demand that would occur if, for example, citizens were better informed about the program or if changes were made to make the program more accessible or attractive or less expensive for users. The estimation of latent demand can add considerably to the difficulty of program analysis.

The following are some sources of information that can be used to estimate needs:[1]

1. Data on the current past incidence of problems, for example, crime rates, fire rates, and incidence of diseases.

2. Basic demographic information. This may include the number of people of a certain age, sex, residential location, or family income. These raw numbers may be of considerable direct importance for some services; for example, the number of residences in an area helps

---

[1] A discussion of the use of a variety of these sources for estimating recreation needs is provided in U.S. Department of the Interior, Bureau of Outdoor Recreation, *Assessing Public Recreation Needs* (Ann Arbor, Michigan: November 1974).

determine the need for waste collection services. In other cases, this information can be used with other information such as incidence rates. For example, the rate of physical handicaps in children between ages one and four might be multiplied by the projected number of children of those ages to yield an estimate of the number of children likely to need physical therapy.

3. Technical indications of conditions, including assessment of road conditions, water and air quality tests, ratings by trained observers of street cleanliness, and health examination surveys. Such indications can help identify significant problem areas.

4. Data on past *expressed* demand, such as attendance at recreational facilities, number of passenger trips on transit systems, and the number of persons applying for program assistance. Waiting lists can also provide a rough estimate of current unmet needs. However, many potential clients may not be on such lists, while some who are on the lists may not qualify for services.

5. Information from surveys of citizens. For example, a survey asking how many days a person was unable to work for health reasons in the recent past would indicate the magnitude of health problems. Similarly, questions about whether people are satisfied with certain government services might identify needs for improvement.

6. Complaint data. The number of complaints received about a service give some indication of the nature and scope of problems with the service. Complaints will usually come only from a vocal segment of the population, so this information will not necessarily represent the views of a cross-section of the population, as a special survey would. But complaint data can identify trouble spots.

These six sources can provide information on the current magnitude of the incidence and prevalence of various problems. To estimate *future* needs, however, analysts must use techniques similar to those discussed in Chapter 5, such as statistical projections of past data.

One county wanted to know how many elderly persons were

going to need various levels of care. Officials undertook a survey of elderly persons both in and out of institutions. The survey asked many questions about the elderly persons' physical, mental, and social well-being, such as whether they could cook for themselves. The responses were combined to provide estimates of the number of persons needing various levels of care.[2]

Client Difficulty Estimates

As noted in Chapter 5, many estimates of the effectiveness of a program require estimates to be made of effectiveness for different categories of clients. If the mix of clients is changing, overall effectiveness will be affected. This applies not only to human resource programs, but also in one form or other to a wide range of other government programs.

For example, an analyst concerned with police programs may use as measures of effectiveness the crime rate and the proportion of cases that are closed by apprehension of suspects. To gain a valid picture, however, the analysts should set up categories of crimes according to their type and severity to distinguish, for example, between robbery and minor vandalism.

The analyst, thus, needs to project how many cases will fall into each category of difficulty and how effective a program will be for each category. The analysis may find important differences both in the resources needed to deal with each category of cases, and in the effectiveness of the various program alternatives in treating each category.

A Note on Cost-Benefit Analysis

Cost-benefit analysis, as we use the term here, is a special form of analysis in which dollar values are imputed to some or all of the effectiveness criteria. As a result, effects are stated in terms of estimated monetary benefits. In such studies, the analysts generally attempt to infer or impute the monetary value of a benefit, such as the amount of money individuals would be willing to pay to receive

---

[2]Quentin Thompson, "Assessing the Need for Residential Care for the Elderly" (London: Greater London Council Intelligence Unit, Quarterly Bulletin, No. 24, September 1973).

the benefits of a proposed project.[3] These analyses usually do not try to identify the differing effects on different client groups.

Examples of monetary imputations sometimes used in cost-benefit studies are (1) the value of time saved from reduced travel time; (2) the value of a recreation day, (3) the value of extending the life of patients, perhaps based on an estimate of added earnings for the added years of life, and (4) the value of prevented flood damage.[4]

The cost-benefit analysis approach has the advantage of combining several evaluation criteria, which in an analysis would otherwise be expressed in different units, into one unit of outcome—the dollar. If an analysis shows that the dollar benefits would exceed the dollar costs, the project is presumably worthwhile. Alternatives can be readily ranked on a scale showing the ratio between costs and benefits, or a scale showing value of benefits after the costs have been subtracted.

However, the imputations required to translate nonmonetary into monetary units are often quite tenuous. Many program effects do not have meaningful dollar values. The use of dollar values can obscure many important assumptions that should be made explicit for the consideration of decision makers. Therefore, we do not recommend the use of cost-benefit analysis unless it *supplements* a presentation of straightforward evaluation criteria estimates, and then only if the method for making the imputations of dollar value is clearly presented.

Time Period To Be Covered by the Analysis

Analyses that consider only the immediate future, such as the next budget year, often lead to short-sighted decisions. In this respect, it is more desirable to consider costs and effects as far into the future as relevant. On the other hand, the longer the time period involved in the projection, the greater are the uncertainties in the estimates.

---

[3]For a concise account of the concept of cost-benefit analysis, see *Evaluation of Techniques for Cost-Benefit Analysis of Water Pollution Control Programs and Policies.* Report of the Administrator of the Environmental Protection Agency to the Congress of the United States (Washington, D.C.: U.S. Government Printing Office, 1975).

[4]See, for example, Illinois Economic and Fiscal Commission, *Water Resource Management in Illinois: Program Review* (Springfield, Illinois, January 1974).

How many future years should be considered? Unfortunately, there is little scientific guidance on this issue.

The need to consider future years is affected by the extent to which a current decision can be revised at a later date. Analyses that contain alternatives involving substantial capital expenditures for such facilities as fire stations, water or sewage treatment plants, and hospitals have significant long-range implications and are likely to require estimates for perhaps ten or more years. Decisions on procedural matters, such as how to deploy maintenance crews or police patrol units, which do not involve additional staff or facilities, and which can usually be modified more readily, generally require shorter time periods, perhaps two to three years. However, even personnel and procedural changes, such as those in which substantial increases in personnel would be required or where new program constituencies are likely to form rapidly, are at times difficult to reverse or alter. In such cases a longer planning horizon is needed.

The program analyst should consider how long it will take to procure the resources for each alternative, how long it will take to implement the program once resources are in place, and how long the program will operate. A reasonable length of time should be allowed. For example, in the analysis of a drug treatment program, summarized in Appendix A-3, analysts looked at the effectiveness of the program over five years in order to allow for start-up time—hiring staff, obtaining a facility, and attracting and selecting patients—and to allow the program to stabilize so that the cost and effectiveness figures would properly reflect the impacts of clients in various phases of treatment.

Generally the time period for any projection should be long enough so that costs and long-term benefits can stabilize or reach a recurring cycle. If decision makers are likely to be concerned about the cost of an initial investment, the analysis should cover the time likely to be needed to pay back the investment. For some program options, such as an extension of an existing program, this may be only one or two years. For those involving new programs with new concepts or new construction, this may be at least five or ten years.

The length of the projected time period should also allow for a consideration of possible significant changes in conditions that could alter the attractiveness of an alternative. A key question often will be how long it will take for the alternative to become obsolete because of technologies or because of a change in the clients. For example, projected rates of community growth could alter the need for various public facilities. Obviously, this should be considered in making current facility decisions. In a fire station location analysis, for example, analysts constructed a model with the city configured as the planners projected it for 1980 as well as for the current period. Investment and operating costs were considered for each alternative.[5]

Some "future" considerations occasionally overlooked in program analyses follow:

1. New facilities and equipment carry substantial maintenance costs. Estimated savings may be overstated if future maintenance costs, particularly those for complex new facilities or equipment, are not considered.

2. It usually takes time for new programs to shake down and become fully operational. Estimates of near-future program performance are likely to be overstated if this is not considered.

3. Programs involving personnel reductions are likely to encounter delays before full savings are realized so that personnel reductions can be achieved through attrition or transfers, rather than by dismissals.

4. The effects of future inflation on salaries, costs of equipment, and prices of land may considerably escalate program costs, especially for items involving extended lead time. This is especially important where different program options involve different phasing or mixes of cost items with differing inflation factors.

5. Demand or need for a program can change in the future, as can the types of clients to be served. Such changes can affect the impact of program options.

Considering Uncertainty

Estimates of future conditions in which programs will operate, of future program effectiveness, and of future program costs are

---

[5]International City Management Association, *Applying Systems Analysis in Urban Government: Three Case Studies* (Washington, D.C., March 1972).

inherently uncertain. Use of sound techniques and the best available existing data for developing such estimates should improve the quality of the estimates. But by no means will this remove the uncertainty.

A program analysis should identify the major uncertainties and, to the extent feasible, identify their magnitudes and implications for program decisions. This will require careful consideration of the linkage between proposed program features and program effectiveness and cost. Unfortunately, very few program analyses have specifically identified and estimated the extent to which uncertainties are present in their findings. A classic example occurs with manpower training programs. Training does not automatically lead to employment. Estimating only the number of people completing training is not sufficient. Estimates are needed as to the likely availability of jobs at the time training is completed, in those occupations for which the training is supposed to be helpful. Assumptions as to economic and job market conditions—which have their own uncertainties—would be needed.[6]

The analytical problems and available alternatives for estimating and handling uncertainty are in themselves a major and lengthy topic. Some approaches that might be used include the following:

1. Providing estimates of the probabilities of various events or conditions. Depending on the degree of uncertainty, these estimates could be expressed in a precise manner or by using qualitative statements of the degree of likelihood.

2. Estimating how much the results will change in response to possible changes in the major assumptions used in the analysis ("sensitivity analysis"). The analysts would estimate the effects on the cost and effectiveness estimates for each alternative for different assumptions, particularly those subject to major uncertainty.

3. Expressing estimates of cost and effectiveness with ranges of

---

[6]An example of the miscalculation of such availability is provided in one state's program audit on prison vocational training programs. See Commonwealth of Pennsylvania, Office of the Budget, *Program Audit Report on Vocational Training in Pennsylvania State Correctional Institutions* (Harrisburg, Pennsylvania, October 1970).

values rather than a single value. Such ranges might be based on the following: [7]

(a) statistical calculations where statistical sampling was used;
(b) calculations obtained by altering the values of various variables, based on information available to the analysts as to other possible values (especially feasible when computerized mathematical models have been used to help make estimates of costs and effectiveness);
(c) expert judgment.

4. At the very least, providing qualitative statements identifying the major uncertainties and risks involved.

Information on the magnitude of uncertainty in the analysis findings is valuable in the following ways:

First, it warns those using the analytical results about the risks in selecting each program alternative. One of the few examples where uncertainty is often explicitly considered quantitatively in government services occurs in decisions on water supply and drainage facilities. Probabilities of various amounts of rainfall are calculated (based on historical records) and often expressed in such terms as a "once-every-hundred-years rain." The likelihood and risks that various facility capacities will be too small can then be calculated. Decision makers can then make their choices based on the costs and risks involved.

Second, government officials may want to select those alternatives that hold up well under a range of possible "futures" (often termed "robust" alternatives), rather than accept an alternative that might perform extremely well under one possible set of conditions but poorly under other possible conditions. Such information may also encourage the development of new alternatives as "hedges" against the major uncertainties.

Third, if program selection involves inordinate uncertainty and risk, this factor may suggest the need for better, less uncertain

---

[7]This effort can become quite technically sophisticated. For example, some efforts have been made to obtain quantitative estimates of the "highest likely," "most likely," and "least likely" values for individual cost or effectiveness elements from experts. Based on assumed probability distributions for the actual values of each element (such as the Beta distribution used for PERT estimates in scheduling), all these elements would then be combined into total cost or effectiveness estimates. This would produce an expected value and "confidence intervals" for the totals.

information—perhaps by more extensive data collection or by undertaking pilot projects—prior to decision making.

Many analysts warn against presenting findings without providing adequate information about the nature and degree of uncertainty present in the findings. Unfortunately, this aspect continues to be neglected. Time and resource restraints, the desire of analysis users for simple, easy-to-grasp findings, and technical difficulties in making additional estimates conspire to discourage the explicit consideration of uncertainty. With such realities, we suggest that at the least each program analysis be required to contain a statement on the nature and magnitude of the uncertainties, even if it is only a brief paragraph concerning the degree to which a user can have confidence in the figures presented.

Chapter 7
Implementation Feasibility:
A Special Aspect of
Program Analysis

Program analyses seldom adequately discuss the feasibility of putting the various alternatives into operation. Typically, they assume that each alternative would be equally easy to set up and operate in the approximate form developed by the analysis. However, implementation problems can increase the cost of the selected alternative, decrease its effectiveness, create delay, and even prevent the selected alternative from being used.

Government policy makers inevitably consider feasibility of implementation (explicitly or implicitly) as an additional criterion in making their decisions. Thus, a systematic, explicit treatment of this issue seems called for in order to:

1. Identify possible implementation impacts on cost and program effectiveness, including timing, so that estimates provided in the analysis are more realistic;

2. Provide a comparison of the feasibility of implementing various alternatives and alert public officials to special efforts needed to implement them; and

3. Suggest means by which implementation might be eased by revising alternatives.

Since program analyses have seldom explicitly examined implementation feasibility, any attempt to outline systematic procedures for doing so has little precedent. There are, however, a few documented case studies that can be called upon.[1] Though it is beyond the scope of this work to give a full treatment to this subject, some initial suggestions can be presented.

Exhibit 21 contains a checklist of conditions affecting implementation feasibility. The degree to which any of these conditions can be identified is not clear. It will be impossible for analysts to predict all implementation hurdles, including the "hidden agendas" that inevitably appear in such situations. The factors are based on the authors' own judgments and observations and have been developed without the benefit of actual study of the extent to which each is actually related to implementation difficulty. Additional research on this matter is obviously needed.

What Might Analysts Do Regarding the Implementation Feasibility Issue?

There are a number of different roles for the analyst in Implementation Feasibility ("IF") analysis:

1. *At a minimum, analysts should attempt to indicate the potential impacts of implementation difficulties on the costs and effectiveness of each alternative.* Possible delays in implementation also should be identified. Analysts and the proposers of alternatives too often minimize the amount of lead time required for approval and implementation of alternatives. The findings of analysis generally are not sensitive to delays of a few months in implementation. However, implementation can be delayed for many months, or even years; and

---

[1]See, for example: Martha A. Derthick, *New Towns In-Town: Why a Federal Program Failed* (Washington, D.C.: The Urban Institute, 1972); Jeffrey L. Pressman and Aaron B. Wildavsky, *Implementation* (Berkeley: University of California Press, 1973); James L. Sundquist, with the collaboration of David W. Davis, *Making Federalism Work* (Washington, D.C.: The Brookings Institution, 1969).

In addition, as of this writing, faculty at such schools as the Harvard University John F. Kennedy School and the Stanford University Business School have been developing teaching programs on analysis for implementation. We are indebted to Erwin C. Hargrove for his identification of these relevant published materials as well as for his guidance on this chapter. His paper, "The Missing Link: The Study of Implementation," (Washington, D.C.: The Urban Institute, July 1975) lays out many of the research issues in government implementation problems.

In addition to the case studies, see Anthony Downs, *Inside Bureaucracy*, RAND Corporation Research Study (Boston: Little Brown and Co., 1967), a well-known discussion of the closely related issue of "bureaucratic behavior." Most of the cases included in the items referenced above deal primarily with federal programs but involve local efforts. However, similar problems are likely to be encountered at all levels of government.

such possible delays should be identified explicitly and considered by analysts in their estimates of costs and program effectiveness.

2. *The analysis might identify and attempt to quantify the main implementation difficulties of each alternative.* Exhibit 21 could be helpful as a checklist for this purpose. This information could be used as an additional criterion for making program choices. The following two approaches might be used:

Alternatives might be ranked. For example, "Alternative A is likely to be more difficult to implement than Alternatives B and C," "Alternative C is more difficult than D," etc.

Alternatives might be rated, perhaps using "expert" judgment or some arbitrary scale to yield an implementation feasibility score. For example, Alternative A may be rated as "very difficult" or given a numerical rating of 10 on a scale of 1 to 10 in order of increasing difficulty. Alternative B might be rated as "difficult" and given a rating of 7. Alternative C might be rated as the "least difficult to implement" and given a rating of 3.

In both approaches, each of the implementation factors, such as those listed in Exhibit 21, could be rated or ranked.

Such ratings present numerous difficulties. However, if the procedure were understandable and made clear to users, and if the component ratings for each factor, as well as the overall rating, were also presented, the likelihood of being misleading would be substantially reduced.

In estimating the implementation feasibility of the various alternatives, it is likely to be appropriate to use individuals familiar with the administrative and political environment.

3. *Analysts or officials might try to develop variations of the alternatives that would make implementation more feasible.* This would be done after considering the major implementation hurdles. However, the analysts should not eliminate alternatives because of major obstacles to implementation. Decision makers themselves should decide whether the alternative is worth the effort. Thus, the potential costs and effectiveness of major alternatives, even those with substantial apparent implementation difficulties, should be examined. In the design of variations to ease implementation of an alternative, careful attention should be paid to possible added costs and reduced effectiveness introduced in the attempt.

Exhibit 21.   FACTORS TO EXAMINE IN ASSESSING
IMPLEMENTATION FEASIBILITY OF EACH
PROGRAM ALTERNATIVE.

1. *How many agencies [both internal and external to the government] must cooperate or participate in order to ensure successful implementation?* In some cases, agencies of other governments or components of the private sector (such as business concerns or citizen groups)might be involved. Since such groups are not responsible to the governmental unit, their actions may render any given alternative infeasible. The more people and groups that are required to provide approval or support, the more difficult implementation is likely to be. External agencies might be weighted more than internal agencies in estimating implementation difficulty.

2. *To what extent does the alternative directly affect services in a way clearly visible to the public? Are there existing client groups whose interests will be affected, particularly by a cutback in existing services?* Alternatives that propose maintaining or increasing existing levels of services will be less likely to present implementation difficulties than ones that reduce the level of service. For example, the choice of different types of refuse collection vehicles will probably be less controversial than the question of whether refuse should be collected at the curb instead of at the back door.

3. *To what extent does the alternative threaten important officials by reductions in power, prestige, or privileges?* Such individuals, of course, can be expected to resist implementation.

4. *To what extent does the alternative threaten jobs?* Especially where a strong employees' organization is present, opposition can be great. Special compensation might be required to gain acceptance. Estimated cost savings may be considerably less than initially estimated.

5. *To what extent are special personnel capabilities required?* Will additional training be required? Are needed personnel likely to be available and obtainable within the existing civil service system? If not, can special provisions be made for obtaining such personnel?

6. *To what extent does the alternative require changes in the behavior of governmental employees?* Employees may be unable or

Exhibit 21. (continued)

unwilling to behave as intended by the alternative. For example, an alternative may involve assumptions about police officers' behavior towards suspected criminals or the care with which solid waste collectors handle containers. Or it may require different working hours or location of employees, all of which might lead to resistance.

7. *Are the sources of funds and their availability fairly definite? To what extent does the alternative call for added amounts of funds in the face of tight revenue constraints?* Some sources of funds may be more likely to be realized than others. Alternatives involving special funding support may be subject to considerable' uncertainties. An alternative that requires bond issue approval is likely to encounter considerable uncertainty and lengthy delays.

8. *Are there complicated legal questions, and if so, are changes such as new legislation required? What is the likelihood that these changes would be made?* At the very least, this factor will probably impose delays.

9. *To what extent has public debate galvanized opinions for or against the alternative?*

10. *To what extent does the alternative require space or facilities that may be difficult to obtain?* For example, neighborhood populations may resist locating drug treatment centers, mental health facilities, nursing homes, half-way homes, etc., in their neighborhoods.

11. *To what extent does the alternative involve significant technological uncertainties?* New technologies typically involve operational problems that may increase costs, reduce effectiveness, and delay or even prevent implementation.

12. *Has a recent crisis lent support to one of the alternatives?* Implementation problems might be alleviated if the problem is clearly recognized by the community. For example, a recent wave of burglaries might greatly improve the chances of gaining rapid acceptance for more police patrol units. On the other hand, programs that emphasize prevention before a problem is generally recognized tend to be more difficult to sell. (Note, however, that one of the advantages of systematic analysis is the opportunity to identify emerging problems and to produce evidence for encouraging preventive action.)

4. *Program analysis teams should include personnel of the affected agencies or of those that will participate in implementation.* Their involvement in the process of analysis should lead to more feasible alternatives and also make the findings more palatable by relieving the "not-invented-here" problem.

5. *Analysts might themselves participate in the early stages of implementation,* since implementation often gives rise to problems that were not recognized in the analysis. This reduces the likelihood that the analysts will make the same omission in the future.

Who Should Do the Implementation Feasibility Analysis?

Some jurisdictions may prefer to consider analysis of feasibility as an activity completely separate from the basic program analysis, perhaps on the assumption that different kinds of personnel are required. This might cause the loss of one advantage of implementation feasibility analysis, namely that of alerting program analysts to certain realistic implications of the alternatives. Many, if not most, program analysts are oriented toward quantitative measurement, and they are likely to feel uncomfortable with the more qualitative analysis of feasibility. However, the systematic approach of the program analyst should be useful in feasibility studies.

Some Final Comments

One problem that could inhibit formal implementation feasibility analysis is the sensitive nature of the analysis itself. Because government analyses inevitably become public, candid implementation information could cause problems among various interest groups. However, if a proper, nonmanipulative tone is used throughout the analysis, this problem may be alleviated.

Finally, as indicated at the beginning of this chapter, the ideas presented have not been tested to any extent. Because of this, they must be considered as suggestive and not definitive.

Appendix A
Program Analysis Illustrated: Three Case Studies

This appendix illustrates the procedures of program analysis by summarizing three actual analyses, conducted jointly by personnel from the governments involved and The Urban Institute.

The three cases are not examples of ideal program analysis. Each analysis had shortcomings, typical of those likely to be encountered by government: limited resources, limited time, and limited data. However, in each case the topic was considered important by government officials, and each analysis affected subsequent decisions.

These cases are not true tests of the ability of governments to make program analyses independently, because outside personnel were involved. They do, however, indicate what governments themselves may undertake.

Each case study describes briefly the environment in which the study was made, steps taken, technical approaches used, and actual impacts of the analyses. Each has the following organization:

A. Background and size of the analytic effort
B. Summary of the analysis. The following approximate format is used (some modifications have been made in each case to highlight special features):
    1. Identification of objectives and evaluation criteria
    2. Examination of the magnitude of the problem ("needs assessment")
    3. Identification of options
    4. Estimation of effectiveness of each option
    5. Estimation of the cost of each option
    6. Summarization of the findings on the cost and effectiveness of the options (the analysis of neglected

and dependent children also included an examination of revenue sources and estimated amounts, a step that is likely to be appropriate on occasion)
C. Impact of the analysis
D. Miscellaneous considerations

Two analyses were of human resource programs, which have not always been considered susceptible to quantitative analysis. All three analyses were conducted by local governments. However, the steps taken and the problems encountered should be similar in state governments. Furthermore, the two human resource analyses deal with services often provided by state governments.

Appendix A-1
Options for Improving
Short-term Care of Neglected
and Dependent Children[1]

Background and Size of the Analytic Effort

This was an analysis for Metropolitan Nashville-Davidson County, Tennessee, of alternative ways to improve the short-term care of neglected and dependent (N-D) children, from the time a petition is filed with the Juvenile Court declaring a child to be neglected and dependent until the court's disposition. The analysis was sponsored by the mayor's office of Nashville-Davidson County. The project used part-time personnel from the mayor's office and the local Urban Observatory, one person from the county social service agency, and two members of The Urban Institute (each half-time). In addition, throughout the analysis the mayor's fiscal administrative assistant provided informal guidance. The study was made over a period of about eight months in 1970. It required approximately two person-years of effort, with about half of this time devoted to data gathering and processing.

The problem was identified by the mayor's assistant, who felt that improvements in the existing system were needed. He had to decide in the near future whether to enlarge Richland Village, the county's children's home, where more than half of the N-D children

---

[1]For a full description of the analysis, see Marvin R. Burt and Louis Blair, *Options for Improving the Care of Neglected and Dependent Children* (Washington, D.C.: The Urban Institute, March 1971).

were placed while awaiting court disposition. Personnel in the welfare agencies and in the mayor's office felt that the short-term care system was not working as it should.

The scope of the study was limited to short-term care. It excluded care after court disposition, though the latter was also a concern of the mayor's assistant. Examining long-term care as well as short-term care in any depth was felt to require more resources and time than were available for the study.[2]

Children could be classified as neglected and dependent when no one was readily available to care for them properly. Frequent causes of such classification included the hospitalization of parents, severe physical abuse or neglect by parents, abandonment, incarceration of parents, and emotional difficulty. Parents, relatives, neighbors, police, welfare workers, or the children themselves could file petitions (requests for care) at the intake office of the Juvenile Court. An intake officer was on duty 24 hours a day to accept petitions. However, at the time of the study, intake officers made no attempt to determine whether the petition *should* be filed. After the petition was filed, the intake officer would place the child temporarily pending Juvenile Court disposition. If there was no clearly available and appropriate place for the child to stay (such as with relatives), the child was generally placed temporarily at Richland Village, or in an emergency foster shelter if he was less than three years old. After an average of two to three weeks (as found by the analysis), the child's case was heard in the Juvenile Court. In 1969 N-D petitions were filed for 630 different children; 330 of them were placed temporarily at Richland Village.

Summary of the Analysis

Step 1: Identification of program objectives and evaluation criteria. The main objectives in this analysis were (1) reducing the number of children subjected to the system by screening out cases in which special care was not needed; (2) keeping the child in his home, or at least in a family environment, whenever possible, rather than placing the child in an institution, which is often traumatic for the child; and (3) minimizing the costs of achieving these objectives.

---

[2]Actually, in the analysis, a brief examination was made of longer term care options. This is described in the reference report.

The principal evaluation criteria used were (1) the number of different children named in N-D petitions, (2) the number of children kept in homelike environments rather than institutionalized, and (3) estimated program costs.

Step 2. Examination of the flow of children through the system. As in many program analyses, information readily available at the beginning was inadequate for identifying the major characteristics and the effectiveness of the existing system. Intake and court records were examined for the preceding year, 1969, to determine the number of N-D petitions and the reasons for them, where the children were kept prior to the court hearing, and what the final court dispositions were. The flow diagram shown in Exhibit A-1 illustrates some of the findings. The study found that 180 of the 630 children (28 percent) were brought into the system on petitions that were later withdrawn (there was no court hearing, and they returned to their homes); 332 were placed temporarily at Richland Village, and about 60 percent of these were later sent home. These findings raised substantial questions as to whether the children should have been taken from their homes in the first place. Although there was 24-hour intake of children, the process did not include screening and did not provide emergency services in homelike environments.

Step 3. Identification of options for improving the system's performance. Analysts identified five subprograms that were potentially feasible and worth analyzing. These options were developed on the basis of a careful assessment of needs, discussions with welfare workers, and communication with the federal government and other cities. They follow:

1. *Twenty-four-hour intake screening.* A Welfare worker would be on call round-the-clock to investigate each case and determine whether there were appropriate grounds for filing a petition. If so, the worker would decide how best to care for the child until court disposition.

2. *Emergency caretaker service.* An emergency caretaker would enter the child's home as a custodian, usually staying only overnight. This would be especially effective in cases of temporary abandonment, when parents were delayed in returning home.

108

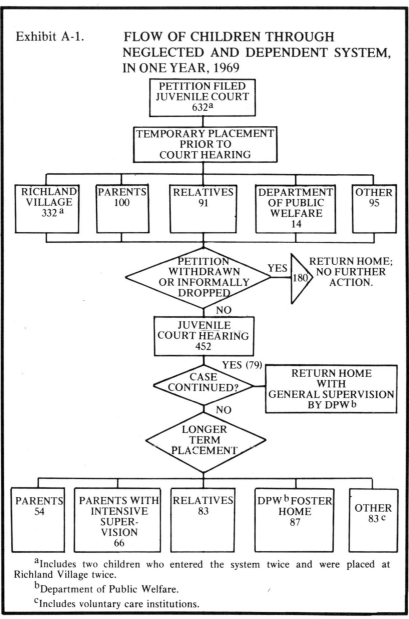

Exhibit A-1.   FLOW OF CHILDREN THROUGH
NEGLECTED AND DEPENDENT SYSTEM,
IN ONE YEAR, 1969

PETITION FILED
JUVENILE COURT
632[a]

TEMPORARY PLACEMENT
PRIOR TO
COURT HEARING

| RICHLAND VILLAGE 332[a] | PARENTS 100 | RELATIVES 91 | DEPARTMENT OF PUBLIC WELFARE 14 | OTHER 95 |

PETITION WITHDRAWN OR INFORMALLY DROPPED

YES 180 → RETURN HOME; NO FURTHER ACTION.

NO

JUVENILE COURT HEARING 452

CASE CONTINUED?

YES (79) → RETURN HOME WITH GENERAL SUPERVISION BY DPW[b]

NO

LONGER TERM PLACEMENT

| PARENTS 54 | PARENTS WITH INTENSIVE SUPERVISION 66 | RELATIVES 83 | DPW[b] FOSTER HOME 87 | OTHER 83[c] |

[a]Includes two children who entered the system twice and were placed at Richland Village twice.

[b]Department of Public Welfare.

[c]Includes voluntary care institutions.

Source: Marvin R. Burt and Louis H. Blair, *Options for Improving
the Care of Neglected and Dependent Children* (Washington, D.C.: The Urban Institute, March 1971), p. 33.

3. *Homemaker service.* Trained homemakers, able to give many days of care, would be used to maintain children in the children's homes during the crisis period.

4. *Emergency foster homes.* Emergency foster homes would be used to maintain the children in family environments where it was not feasible to keep them in their own homes prior to their Juvenile Court hearing.

5. *County children's home.* Under the existing system this was the usual destination for children on whom a petition was filed. The other options would tend to reduce the number of children sent to the home for short-term care.

Nashville already was using emergency foster homes for children less than three years old and a small amount of homemaker service. The emergency caretaker service and the intake screening system would be completely new activities.

These options are not mutually exclusive; four combinations of them were considered as alternatives. Exhibit A-2 summarizes the four alternatives considered in the analysis. All included 24-hour screening and emergency caretaker service. Alternatives I and II combined options 1 through 4 so that all children likely to need the various services (based on the 1969 caseload) would receive them. Alternative I stressed homemaker service, and Alternative II stressed foster homes. Alternatives III and IV featured lower levels of these two services than I and II, but included substantially more services than were currently provided.

Step 4. Estimation of effectiveness of each option. The analysts made a critical assumption: that the caseload would be the same in future years as in 1969—about 630 children per year.[2]

The method for estimating the effectiveness of each alternative was based on a detailed analysis of how the 630 cases in 1969 would have been handled under each available new program, as discussed in the following paragraphs.

---

[2]With more time and resources the study might have attempted to make better estimates of future caseloads, or at least to determine how effective the given alternatives would be if the clientele mix were different than in 1969 (to help determine the sensitivity of the program decision to possible deviations from the projected client mix).

Exhibit A-2.   INTAKE AND EMERGENCY CARE—
ALTERNATIVE PROGRAM COMBINATIONS

	Current program (1969)	Alternative (change from current program)			
		I	II	III	IV
24-hour screening	No	Yes	Yes	Yes	Yes
Emergency caretaker	No	Yes	Yes	Yes	Yes
Number of emergency foster homes	2[a]	+5	+13	+5	0
Number of homemakers	13[b]	+30	+15	+4	0
Children placed at Richland Village	469[c]	-325	-325	-167	-37

[a] Used for both N-D children and non-N-D children.
[b] Used only for non-N-D children.
[c] Includes 137 voluntary placements where N-D petitions were not filed; many of these children would be served under Alternatives I, II, and III.

Source: Marvin R. Burt and Louis H. Blair, *Options for Improving the Care of Neglected and Dependent Children* (Washington, D.C.: The Urban Institute, March 1971), p. 22.

Expert judgment by a social worker, based on a detailed examination of each case, was used to predict the effectiveness of 24-hour screening. For each 1969 case, the social worker made a judgment as to whether the petition would have been screened out if the option they examined had been in place. Estimating conservatively, the analysts felt that more than half of the temporary placements could have been avoided.

The case-by-case examination also revealed that in many cases in which the petition was *not* dropped, a trained caseworker could have prevented it from being filed. Of the 630 cases examined, it was estimated that petitions could have been avoided in at least 180, and perhaps as many as 400, cases.

Similarly, for the emergency foster home, homemaker, and emergency caretaker options, the social worker made a detailed review of each of the cases from 1969. Expert judgments were made as to which cases could have been appropriately handled by each of these new options. As is often the case, the analysis indicated that in the homemaker option the returns would diminish as additional homemakers were added. Based on the timing and duration of the 275 cases suitable for homemaker services in 1969, it was estimated that 4 homemakers could have handled 34 percent of the likely cases, 15 could serve 92 percent, but 22 homemakers would be required to handle all the estimated cases. The additional homemakers would increase coverage by only 8 percent, and they would work only when there was a sudden influx of children needing care.

Analysts did not attempt to determine the degree and nature of the uncertainties likely in estimating the number of children flowing through the system on the effectiveness of the services. They could, for example, have used such techniques as sensitivity analysis (see Chapter 6) to indicate how various changes in the number of children and the effectiveness of each sub-program would have affected the estimated overall effectiveness of each alternative. This was a shortcoming of the program analysis.

Step 5. Estimation of the costs of the various alternatives. The cost elements, such as caseworker salaries, were straightforward. The analysts assumed that personnel costs would rise by 10 percent because of increases in wages and employee benefits in the following year. In addition, the 24-hour intake screening personnel would probably incur overtime premiums. Transportation costs for many of the workers and cost of supplies needed by persons entering homes as caretakers or homemakers had to be estimated. For the emergency caretaker service, which was new to Nashville, costs were obtained for a similar service rendered in Buffalo, New York, and adjusted for the size of the Nashville program. Costs for supervisory help also were included where appropriate.

The proposed alternatives also involved *reductions* in an existing service—the Richland Village Children's Home. The analysts estimated the reduction in child-years under each option (see Exhibit A-3), paying particular attention to the cost savings that would result from these reductions. The investigators examined the cost elements at Richland Village to determine which were fixed and which varied with reductions in child-years. Some costs, such as debt service for the cottages, were fixed; others, such as food and clothing, appeared to vary in direct proportion to the number of children. However, about two-thirds of the costs were identified as "semivariable," that is, they decreased with the child load, but not in direct proportion to it. These costs included most of the staffing costs, which decreased as the number of residential cottages was reduced.

6. *Summarization of the effectiveness and costs of the various alternatives.* This is illustrated in Exhibit A-3. The analysts estimated costs and effectiveness both for the initial year (including a six-month startup period) and for a second year, which was assumed to have the same rate of effectiveness as the first year. All costs shown are net after the estimated cost reductions to the county's children's home.

Step 7. Examination of revenue sources. As is the case of many health and welfare programs, the Nashville N-D program was financed by a complicated mixture of federal, state, and local funds. For example, the children's home was financed entirely by local funds, whereas some of the foster home program was financed under the Aid for Dependent Children (AFDC) program. Complicating the situation were changes in federal financing. Possible financing alternatives were also calculated and presented. Though the cost line in Exhibit A-3 shows the combined costs to all governments, of most interest to the government undertaking the analysis is its own share. These were calculated in the analysis, and are roughly proportional to the figures shown for the totals.

Step 8. Examinations of implementation feasibility. The analysts considered only financial aspects of each alternative's feasibility,

Exhibit A-3 EFFECTIVENESS AND COSTS OF SHORT-TERM ALTERNATIVES

Evaluation Criteria	Alternative I		Alternative II		Alternative III		Alternative IV	
	First Year[a]	Second Year[b]	First Year[a]	Second Year[b]	First Year[a]	Second Year[b]	First Year[a]	Second Year[b]
1. Children screened out by 24-hour screening	90-200	180-400	Same as Alternative I		Same as Alternative I		90	180
2. Children avoiding institutional care through use of emergency caretaker	12-25	25-50	Same as Alternative I		Same as Alternative I		12-25	25-50
3. Children avoiding institutional care through use of emergency foster homes	36	73	89	179	36	73	0	0
4. Children avoiding institutional care through use of homemaker	126	252	73	146	47	94	0	0
5. Reduction in Children placed at Richland Village[c],[d]	162	325	162	325	83	167	18	37
Costs ($000)—Federal, state, and local	106	179	78	124	19	13	12	16

[a]Based on six months program development time and only six months operating time.

[b]Also applies to the third and following years.

[c]The 1969 cases examined indicate that most of these children would also need to be served by foster homes or homemakers. Therefore, the total number of reduced placements at Richland Village is conservatively estimated as the sum of criteria 3 and 4, not 2, 3, and 4.

[d]This amounts to reductions per year starting in the second year of more than 12,400 child-days of care (a child-day is one child for one day) for alternatives I or II, 7,300 for alternative III, and 300 for alternative IV.

Source: Marvin R. Burt and Louis H. Blair, *Options for Improving the Care of Neglected and Dependent Children* (Washington, D.C.; The Urban Institute, March 1971), p. 24.

partly because the researchers did not sense any other major problems. One potential problem was noted, however: the possible difficulty that many workers would not want to work the late hours required by many of the options, particularly when they had to work in neighborhoods considered to be dangerous. This could become a major problem and could increase costs by making necessary more attractive salaries or other compensations. In addition, the analysts did not examine in detail whether the cost savings estimated for the children's home would actually be realized. The possible reluctance of agencies to reduce their staffs was a real possibility.

Impact of the Analysis

The recommendations for the improved 24-hour intake screening and emergency care services were attractive not only to local officials but also to the state and federal agencies that provided demonstration funds for the high-option recommended system (Alternative I). This effort began in 1971 and as of this writing is still under way. Round-the-clock intake screening combined with homemaker and emergency foster home care has been put into action, and efforts have been made to implement the rest of Alternative I.

Nashville has begun a continuing evaluation effort, with the assistance of the Nashville Urban Observatory, to obtain regular feedback on the success of the operation. The reduction in the number of children at the county children's home took place roughly as estimated, but the added space was used for other programs rather than for cost reductions.

Miscellaneous Consideration

Throughout the study, analysts received excellent cooperation from state and county agencies. The analysis involved a number of social service and criminal justice agencies, whose staff members were briefed at various points. The analysis did not threaten any significant group, and apparently most agency people felt the findings to be reasonable. The recommendations did not suggest eliminating any agencies and called for expansion of some programs and introduction of others. The reduction at the children's home was acceptable, perhaps in large part because other uses for the facilities were being contemplated. Net added costs to the local government were very small.

The study falls short of being a fully comprehensive, sophisticated analysis. For example, the estimates of the number and type of children likely to come into the child care system in the future were made roughly. The effectiveness criteria used for evaluating the options did not fully examine the quality of care nor the long-term effects of the short-term care, except by use of crude "proxy" measurements. No estimates of uncertainty in anticipated performance were made.

Nevertheless, it seemed to have been a useful study. It also appeared to be well within the capacity of local governments that choose to apply sufficient resources and provide for a reasonably able analyst to guide the analysis.

Appendix A-2
Analysis of the Use of Police Patrol Cars by Off-Duty Patrol Officers[3]

Background and Size of Analytic Effort

In August 1969 the Indianapolis, Indiana, Police Department instituted a plan whereby a police car was assigned to each patrol officer to drive on and off duty. In the space of one month the number of patrol cars on the streets of Indianapolis quadrupled, and the rate of reported crimes and auto accidents dropped sharply. The plan received substantial publicity, and a story appeared in the February 22, 1970, issue of *Parade* magazine. Several members of the Fort Worth, Texas, City Council read the article, and asked the city manager to investigate the plan and ascertain its usefulness to Fort Worth.

The Fort Worth Research and Budget Department (RBD) undertook the study with the assistance of an Urban Institute research staff member. The RBD consisted of a full-time professional staff of nine, with a director who reported directly to the city manager. The study consumed about six person-months of effort, divided equally between The Urban Institute and the RBD. Police department personnel were not active participants in the analysis, although they provided information and reviewed findings. The study ran from

---

[3]For a full description of the analysis, see Fort Worth Research and Budget Department, "The Use of Police Patrol Cars by Off-Duty Patrolmen" (Fort Worth, Texas, 1970); and Donald M. Fisk, *The Indianapolis Police Fleet Plan* (Washington, D.C.: The Urban Institute, October 1970).

March to September 1970; almost all the effort was expended in the first three months of the period. The informal results were presented in May and the results were presented formally to the city council in September. The total direct cost, which was mostly in salaries, was about $10,000. This includes both city and Urban Institute costs; the city did not pay any of the Institute's cost. There were three principal analysts, two from the Fort Worth RBD and one from The Urban Institute. Fort Worth expenditures came from existing RBD allocations. The main out-of-pocket expense to the city was for travel to Indianapolis to collect needed data.

The training and experience of the analysts varied. The two analysts from Fort Worth were candidates for the master of public administration degree. Neither had been trained in the techniques of quantitative analysis. One had conducted several analytical studies. The analyst from The Urban Institute had extensive training and experience in quantitative analysis but only limited experience in the field of public safety and no prior knowledge of Fort Worth.

Summary of the Analysis

Step 1. Identification of objectives and evaluation criteria. The analysts first prepared an "issue paper" describing the problem and identifying the evaluation criteria. The format was similar to that described in Appendix B. Four evaluation criteria were singled out as potentially important and were the focus of the analysis: reduction of the number of crimes, improvements in crime clearance rates, reduction in the number of automobile accidents, and program cost. Three additional criteria were identified in the initial phases of the analysis—police morale, police public image, and citizen fear of crime. These last factors, however, were only briefly addressed in the analysis because of the difficulty of measuring the likely impact of the plan. Though such data could have been obtained by surveys of police and citizens, such surveys had not been taken in Indianapolis; thus "before" and "after" comparisons were not possible.

An estimate was presented for one other measure, "increased time available for patrol." While not an explicit objective of the plan, it is one that is used by police departments and is a useful proxy or surrogate measure of the plan's effect. In Indianapolis, the plan permitted patrol officers to remain longer on their beats because cars no longer had to be transferred at the end of each shift. In addition, servicing of the cars was handled by officers during off-duty hours.

Similar operations were assumed for Fort Worth, and the resulting increase in time available for on-duty patrol was calculated.

Two other considerations helped set limits to the scope of the analysis. First obtaining enough information to substantially reduce the major uncertainties surrounding the plan (for example, its effect on crime rates) would have required resources that the study group lacked. This prompted the analysts to include as one alternative a Fort Worth experiment. Second, time in which to prepare the study was limited. The analysis began in March and the city manager called for a draft report on May 1. While not a serious problem, day-to-day budget operations sometimes interfered with the investigation and the meeting of the deadline, particularly in the early part of the study.

Step 2. Identification of alternatives. Analysts considered four variations on the off-duty use of patrol cars:

1. Provide a car for each city patrol officer living in the county;

2. Provide a car only for patrol officers living in the city;

3. Conduct an experiment on the plan's impact in Fort Worth to reduce uncertainties about the plan's local impact, and

4. Await further results of the plan as used in other jurisdictions.

Other alternatives, such as increased street lighting, additional police, and improved communications, could have been formulated to satisfy the objectives and evaluation criteria listed above. However, analyzing these alternatives was considered beyond the resources and time available. This analysis, then, should be considered a very narrowly focused study.

Step 3. Estimation of costs. Since virtually no information was available in Fort Worth on how the plan operated in Indianapolis, a program evaluation of the Indianapolis experience was chhosen as the best first step. The analysis started with the formulation of a series of hypotheses as to how the plan might affect each of the objectives noted above. A trip to Indianapolis was made, and the readily available statistics were collected for each of these objectives. Because of the timing of the study only a few months of experience were available; initial estimates were based on data through January 1970. These were later updated. (No appreciable change in the findings was noted. Particular attention was given to comparing statistics from before and after the initiation of the plan.[4] Changes which seem to be significant and attributable to the introduction of the plan in Indianapolis were used to estimate the impact in Fort Worth.

Total costs were estimated for each alternative, drawing on Fort Worth and Indianapolis experience. Such factors as initial car cost and cost per mile driven were taken from Fort Worth municipal garage statistics. Factors such as miles driven while off duty and accident rates were adapted from Indianapolis experience. Because of the uncertainty of some of the inputs, particularly that for added mileage driven while off duty (paid for by the government under the plan), a number of different estimates were made using a variety of assumptions. Both capital and operating expenses were identified and estimated for each of the next six fiscal years to indicate the impact of Fort Worth's annual budgets. This was important, since costs tended to bunch in certain years because of the phasing of car purchases.

Step 4: Estimation of effectiveness. The analysts derived estimates for the Fort Worth fleet plan from the experience in Indianapolis. They first made estimates of the number of crimes, clearance rates, and traffic accidents that would have been expected to occur in Indianapolis if the plan had not been introduced.

They arrived at these estimates, based on historical trends, by two procedures. First, they calculated the average annual change of the historical data. This average was added to the data for the year preceding implementation of the plan to provide an estimate for 1969-70. Second, the analysts used a statistical regression analysis to determine the trend line that best fit the historical data. This line was then compared to the actual data. The significance of the differences between actual and projected data was assessed by a standard statistical test.

For example, reported auto thefts declined 22 percent from the projected trend in Indianapolis. A drop of this size is unlikely to have resulted from simple chance factors; while it is not certain that the reduction was due to the introduction of the plan, no other factors were identified to account for the decrease.

---

[4]See Donald M. Fisk, *The Indianapolis Police Fleet Plan* (Washington, D.C.: The Urban Institute, October 1970).

The apparent changes in crime and traffic accidents in Indianapolis after introduction of the plan were considered to be the best available estimate of what was likely to happen to auto thefts if the plan was introduced into Fort Worth. However, there were many uncertainties in the Indianapolis figures as well as additional questions in using these as projections for Fort Worth. The Fort Worth city analysts did not feel comfortable with the specific estimates and chose not to provide in their final report specific quantitative estimates as to how the plan would affect crime. The report did state that no change should be expected in crimes of passion, indoor crime, and percent of crimes cleared.

Also, as noted above, an estimate was made of the increased time available for patrol. Like the Indianapolis plan, the Fort Worth operation assumed that patrol officers would remain on their patrol beats longer because they did not have to transfer the cars at the end of each shift.

Step 5. Examination of implementation feasibility. An attempt was made to consider the feasibility of implementation in Fort Worth. Patrol officers were quizzed as to whether they would be interested in taking home a marked car if the plan were implemented, and the city attorney was asked to comment on any legal implications.

More than 90 percent of the patrol officers indicated a desire to participate if the plan was implemented. The city attorney expressed doubts as to whether giving police officers cars for their personal use was legal under the Texas constitution; however, there was a precedent elsewhere in Texas for this type of plan.

Step 6: Summary of analysis findings.

Alternative 1—A car for each patrol officer living in the county. This option would cost approximately $900,000 the first year of operation and $400,000 each year thereafter. The Fort Worth police budget was about $5.5 million, so this alternative would have increased the budget about 7 percent. It would boost the number of police cars from 102 to 307 and increase the patrol beat activity about 4 percent, or the equivalent of adding twelve full-time patrol officers. It was estimated that automobile accidents would decrease to about 10 percent below the estimated trend. Although Fort Worth analysts decided not to include any specific quantitative estimates of the impact on crime, the report noted the apparent favorable effect in

Indianapolis on outside crime, particularly auto theft, and the apparent lack of effect in other crime areas.

Alternative 2—A car for each patrol officer living within the city limits. This alternative would cost about $500,000 for the first year of operation and $100,000 each year thereafter. It would boost the number of patrol cars to 240 and provide an increase of approximately 3 percent in patrol officers' time for beat activities. Whereas, alternative 1 subsidized a great deal of off-duty driving outside the city limits, this option would restrict all driving to within the city. Thus the net impact on crime and accident rates in the city would not differ much from that noted for alternative 1.

Alternative 3—An experiment with a Fort Worth-based plan. This alternative, which would attempt to resolve some of the uncertainties surrounding the effects and cost of operating a full-scale plan in Fort Worth, was estimated to cost less than $60,000 for a one-year test. Two parts of the city would be matched. Thirty cars would be provided patrol officers in one part, with the other part used as a control group and no cars provided to off duty police officers living in that part. Results would be assessed after one year. The results of this experiment would dictate whether a full-fledge "take-home" plan should be implemented.

Alternative 4—Continuing examination of the plan as used in other jurisdictions. Given the uncertainties associated with the plan, this alternative proposed simply following the experience in Indianapolis and elsewhere to see if strong evidence in favor of the plan became available.

Impact of the Analysis

The city manager and the police chief were kept up-to-date on the study's progress. In mid-May the city manager was given a report on the value of the fleet plan in Indianapolis and some estimates of the plan's cost if operated in Fort Worth. The manager tentatively decided to recommend against adoption in Fort Worth and so indicated informally to the City Council. At this time budget preparation began. Priorities and funds were worked out, first within City Hall and later in the Council. No one pushed for adoption of the plan. The public safety director and the chief of police had higher priorities. At the Council budget hearings, the issue was not raised.

In September, when the budget had been completed, the city manager had the summary report printed and presented to the Council. The report included his recommendation that Fort Worth should continue to monitor the plan's impact in Indianapolis. The Council's action was restricted to a single member's request for a meeting with the public safety director and police chief to solicit their views. The press reported this action, routinely including the alternatives and the city manager's recommendations. The Council did not take any further action.

Miscellaneous Considerations

The Fort Worth program analysis was conducted in a favorable environment, for the following reasons:

1. Local government officials were accessible to the analysts; the city manager, the director of research and budget, and the police chief were included periodically in the discussions.

2. There was enough time to prepare a simple program analysis. The City Council raised the issue of the plan in late February, work started on the analysis in March, and a first draft was completed in May. The report was sent to the Council in September.

3. Analytical assistance was available from members of the Research and Budget staff and Urban Institute analysts. Any time budget matters interfered with the work of the Fort Worth personnel, The Urban Institute analyst picked up the slack.

4. There was a customer for the analysis. The City Council requested information on the plan, and the city manager ordered the study.

There were few advocates and little pressure to implement the plan, before, during, or after the analysis. The City Council simply requested information on the plan. The police chief, who would have liked to implement the plan, placed other programs first. The city attorney objected to the plan. In addition, program costs were

124

relatively large, and, while taxes could have been raised or other programs cut, either move would have been unpopular. [5]

The press was responsible for bringing the plan to the attention of Fort Worth decision makers. It reported on the analysis at several points, in each case, the reporting was straightforward and honest.

The technical quality of the analysis was probably adequate considering the limited resources. Major failings lay in the estimation of the plan's effectiveness. While this part of the analysis is weak, it did lay out the problems and uncertainties and the experience in Indianapolis. Also, the narrow scope of the analysis, particularly the lack of comparisons with other crime or traffic control approaches, greatly limited the potential for "optimizing" the use of city funds.

The city manager had a number of comments concerning the study:

1. Had the effectiveness data been more positive he probably would have recommended a test of the plan.

2. He and the City Council preferred the presentation of a series of alternatives with pros and cons, such as were included in the analysis, rather than the usual limited approach.

3. He viewed the study as a learning process for his staff, and he felt they benefited by its preparation.

4. He recognized the risks, such as increased press coverage, that accompany this kind of analysis, but did not feel they should be inhibiting.

5. He did not feel that the number of person-months required for the analysis was excessive, given the problem. He was willing to assign his staff to similar studies in the future for this amount of time.

---

[5]This might be contrasted with a situation in which an evaluation is made *after* the program has been introduced. If the evaluation indicates little crime or traffic benefits, difficulties in terminating the plan could be considerable because of the foundation of a constituency for the plan—the police officers receiving the cars.

6. Formal documentation was of secondary concern. His interest centered on facts he could use in formulating his own position and answering questions raised by the City Council.

7. The difference between this analysis and the usual city study is one of depth and range. Normally, fewer options would have been examined, and there would have been less examination of Indianapolis data and less concern with operating and maintenance costs.

8. The problem definition or issue paper phase was quite useful.

There are several ways to look at the value of the Fort Worth analysis. One is to compare the cost of the analysis (about $10,000) with the cost of the proposed plan (alternative 2 would cost about $800,000 over the first three years plus about $100,000 annually thereafter); by this standard the analysis seems inexpensive. Another is to rely on the value judgments of the decision makers. The city manager and the director of research and budget gave a qualified yes to the question of whether the analysis was worth the effort. A third is to compare the action resulting from the analysis with what would have taken place without it. It is impossible to know what would have happened without the analysis, but the city manager and the director of research and budget suspect that the plan would have been deferred even without the study.

The analysis demonstrates the need for a nationwide clearinghouse for information on innovative local government programs. Many other cities were confronted with the problem of whether the Indianapolis plan was worthwhile. Indianapolis received more than 100 requests for information on its program. A thorough and objective evaluation document, including the cost and impact of the plan, would have been of great use and would have cut the cost and time of the Fort Worth study by one-third to one-half.

Appendix A-3
Analysis of Hard Drug
Treatment Options[6]

Background and Size of Analytic Effort

This relatively complex analysis was sponsored by the County Manager's Office of Metropolitan Dade County, Florida. The analysis team consisted of members of the Community Improvement Program Office (a staff office to the county manager) and members of The Urban Institute. The team did not include representatives of any of the county's drug treatment agencies (either governmental or private); this was later to cause problems.

As often happens, the initial problem expressed by the government was somewhat vague. The county (like most metropolitan areas in the United States) had become increasingly concerned with the problem of drug abuse, particularly the abuse of "hard" drugs. Few systematic analyses of the various aspects of the drug problem were available. Judgment was therefore used to narrow the problem's focus to hard drugs, particularly heroin, and to the treatment of addicts. Drug education and other preventive measures were not included in the study, largely because the analysts believed that very little substantive data on the effectiveness of prevention activities were or could be made available during the study period with the resources available. Also, ways to reduce the supply of heroin were excluded from the study.

---

[6]For a full description of the analysis, see Marvin R. Burt et al., *Dade County Drug Abuse Treatment System Policy Analysis* (Miami, Florida: Office of the County Manager, Metropolitan Dade County, October 1972).

The analysis began in July 1971. It lasted approximately one year. The final report was provided in October 1972 at a time when a recently elected Board of County Commissioners was faced with a number of questions on drug treatment programs. Approximately 2.5 person-years of effort were applied to the study. Much of this effort was extensive special data collection and processing. This part of the effort could be substantially reduced for future analyses if certain data were routinely gathered as recommended by the analysis team.

The analysis encompassed not only the county's own drug treatment programs (primarily methadone detoxification and maintenance programs with some supportive service), but also three private, residential, therapeutic community programs and a private methadone program.

By the end of the analysis, it had become clear that steps to encourage addicts to enter drug treatment programs should be an important part of future government action, and some analysis effort was spent in this direction. In the early part of the analysis, the team came to believe that a particuarly important group to consider were addicts who were arrested, especially those incarcerated, as this group includes many who commit crimes to support their drug habit.

Summary of the Analysis

Step 1: Identification of objectives and evaluation criteria for both existing programs and proposed future programs. As is usually the case, neither the county government nor those operating individual treatment programs had well-articulated objectives or criteria for evaluating their programs. It is particularly important in drug treatment to distinguish two separate objectives: (1) ridding clients of all addictive drugs and (2) reducing the amount of heroin dependency and thereby increasing client self-sufficiency and reducing the number of drug-related crimes. Treatment programs using legal but still addictive drugs such as methadone might perform well on the second objective but by definition could not on the first.

The evaluation criteria were altered somewhat during the course of the study. The initial temptation was to concentrate on dropout rates (or their complement, retention rates). However, since these measures do not directly indicate the degree of subsequent drug usage, the following criteria were used: (1) number of person-months free of heroin use and (2) number of persons and person-months free of all addictive drugs including methadone. The information in the analysis indicated that retention in a treatment program, during which time an individual was completely or at least substantially free of heroin, was a major benefit both to the individual and to the community. Also, some dropouts seem to be at least partly rehabilitated (by either the residential therapeutic communities or methadone programs). On the other hand, graduating from a treatment program does not guarantee permanent rehabilitation; many return to hard drug use. For methadone maintenance programs, a negative side effect is the addiction of those maintained. This was pointed out in the analysis but not used directly as part of the evaluation criteria.

Step 2: Identification of Alternatives. The alternatives were partly generated from initial findings of the analysis. Suggestions were made by officials of public and private drug programs as well. The wide gap between the number of persons in treatment and the estimated total number of addicts seemed to indicate the need for expansion of programs. Three alternatives to then-current program levels were considered. These included different degrees of expansion of the methadone maintenance effort, establishment of habit reduction "quick detoxification" treatment and expansion of the various types of residential therapeutic communities.

In addition, three other major points were raised by the examination of the current system. (1) There did not seem to be effective provisions for bringing treatment to bear on persons passing through the criminal justice system. Thus, possibilities were raised for systematic screening of persons arrested (perhaps through urinalysis) along with encouraging those identified as addicts to submit to treatment, perhaps in lieu of bringing the cases to trial. (2) Some programs had vacancies. This could be due to a number of reasons. A program may not have been known by addicts, may not have been conveniently located, or may have been known but not liked by them (perhaps because of their belief that rules were too stringent). Possibly, the number of addicts might have been overestimated. It seemed appropriate to consider options for attempting to atract clients into existing programs. Such options could be relatively inexpensive. (3) The analysis indicated that treatment programs were not so attractive to blacks or Latins as to whites. Thus, options presented included ways to attract clients living in black and Latin areas of the community.

The analysis focused on near-future options and did not consider possible new treatment approaches such as drug antagonists, which at some point may be developed enough to substantially revise treatment procedures. Nevertheless, such considerations do suggest that program alternatives that involve large, inflexible investments should be avoided if technological advances rendering the program obsolete appear possible. For the most part, the alternatives did not involve such inflexible programs.

Step 3: Estimation of costs. Cost estimation for treatment expansion is not as easy as it may first appear. Cost information was obtainable from the treatment programs, but there were at least two major and not uncommon problems. First, all of the costs actually incurred in running a program were not charged against the program; some costs, such as those for shared services, were charged entirely to other programs, leading to an unrealistically low cost figure. Analysts had to examine the treatment program thoroughly, determine what services were provided, and check accounting records to see if these services were fully charged against the program. When the services had not been adequately charged to the program, analysts had to estimate how much of the cost of these services should be charged to the program. Some items were difficult to handle. For example, the methadone program used rehabilitation specialists whose services were shared with other programs, but fully charged against the methadone program. At first the analysts did not realize the services were shared; they attributed the entire cost of the specialists to the program, greatly overestimating the per person treatment costs. Fortunately, this mistake was identified by the agency concerned during review of the preliminary study findings.

Second, future costs might differ from past costs. The therapeutic communities, for example, sometimes had services or facilities donated. Such donations might not be available for further expansion; the items would then have to be supported by other funds, possibly those of the local government.

Step 4: Estimation of effectiveness. As usual, this was the most difficult task. It consisted of four phases: estimation of the magnitude of the problem (need assessment); a program evaluation of existing county treatment programs; a closely related phase of collection of effectiveness information from similar programs outside Dade County;

and estimation of likely effectiveness of each alternative, using the program evaluation data.

a. *Estimation of the magnitude of the hard drug problem in the county.* An effort was made to identify the size of the gap between the capacity of existing treatment programs and the apparent need, the number of addicts in the community. It is very difficult, if not impossible, to make precise estimates of the total number, since addiction is generally hidden. Adaptations of a formula employed in New York which related the number of addicts to the annual number of reported overdose deaths were used to provide a range of estimates. The range was estimated as between 7,000 and 12,000 addicts in the county. This range was used in the analysis to help determine the amount of treatment capacity to recommend.

Other indicators were also used:

1. Counts of the number of addicts who were or had been enrolled in treatment programs—there were about 1,000 to 1,500 in treatment.

2. Estimates of backlogs of applications for admittance to these programs—a wait of two to three months for admission was typical.

3. The number of deaths due to use of narcotics (obtained from the county medical examiner).

4. The number of arrests on drug charges (obtained from the police department).

5. The percentage of jail inmates who were drug addicts (estimated by examining intake forms for persons admitted to the jail over a three-month period)—it appeared that at least 10 percent of the inmates were addicts.

From the above information and statements obtained from treatment program records about the daily cost of drug habits, analysts made rough estimates of the total value of property stolen. Typical problems with these estimates included the difficulty in estimating how many crimes a person would have committed were he not an addict. Also, information was very scarce about the proportion of heroin paid for with proceeds of crimes against property—burglarly or buying and selling stolen goods—and violent crimes such as robbery, rather than by legal or less violent means such as prostitution and drug dealing.

b. Evaluation of existing county treatment programs. This was the most time-consuming part of the effort. It was first necessary to identify and describe existing drug treatment programs. This was surprisingly difficult because of the many approaches and organizations involved. The focus of the analysis eventually centered on the three major residential therapeutic communities and two methadone detoxification-maintenance programs (the county government's and a private hospital's).

A major concern in examining drug treatment program is that some types of clients are more difficult to rehabilitate than others. Thus, data were sought on the characteristics of the clientele for these programs. Such information as length of addiction, age, sex, and race was obtained on current and former patients of each program. The county's programs had all started in 1969 or after, so there was only limited experience, particularly on graduates. Some programs keep clients eighteen months and even longer (for example, methadone maintenance programs can keep clients indefinitely).

In addition, data on clients' performance while in treatment were obtained, including evidence of drug use, arrests, and dropout rates (and length of time before dropout). Overall statistics were developed on retention rates, failure rates, and arrest rates. These statistics were assumed to hold in the future. The information was obtained on clients from the beginning of the treatment programs until the time of the evaluation. There was some initial reluctance on the part of the programs to provide access to individual records, but with the proper assurances of confidentiality, access was obtained. One program withheld records on one group of patients because of its interpretation of a federal regulation limiting access to client records for a federally funded program. Except for this, information was gathered on all clients. With a larger number of cases, it would have been more practical to sample the cases.

An attempt was made to follow up candidates after they had left a treatment program—whether because of graduation, dropout, or discharge. Follow-ups are needed in such evaluations for obtaining estimates on the longer term effects of treatment. Major difficulties existed. Two programs would not release names, thus preventing follow-up of their clients. As already noted, the treatment programs had not been in existence long enough to have many graduates, although they had many dropouts. In addition, it can be difficult to locate former patients. Limited resources, combined with a late starting date for the interviews, in part caused by the initial reluctance of one of the treatment programs to have its former clients interviewed (as a potential invasion of privacy), prevented a fully satisfactory number of interviews from being conducted. Recent college graduates were used as interviewers. Information was sought in particular on the extent to which the patients had returned to drugs after leaving the program, and their employment status.

One major source of follow-up information was police arrest files. These were checked against the names of patients by the analysis team (to avoid possible violations of confidentiality). Use of arrest record presents a number of problems. For this analysis, only county records were examined; arrests in other jurisdictions were not covered. Not all persons arrested are guilty, and former drug addicts may be particularly likely to be arrested (though that did not seem to be the case in Dade County for the time of the study). On the other hand, many crimes do not lead to arrest. Nevertheless, arrest records provide some basis for indicating subsequent criminal behavior of clients.

Analysts were inadvertently given misleading data on client characteristics from one program, and the mistake was not discovered until the draft of the final report was being reviewed. This would probably not have happened had a representative of that program been an active member of the project team. In another case, project analysts made an error in determining costs because of unfamiliarity with the program. Again, this probably could have been prevented by having program staff as active members of the project team.

c. *Development of effectiveness information from similar programs outside Dade County.* Because of the newness and small size of the Dade County treatment programs, the analysts also obtained information on program retention and rehabilitation rates from analogous large treatment programs in other parts of the country. These data were used both to provide benchmarks against which to evaluate the Dade County programs, as well as to provide data for projecting the performance of similar programs in Dade County. The same rates were anticipated to be achieved in Dade County. Programs in which there seemed to be extensive related experience and data available included the New York Daytop residential therapeutic community and the Washington, D.C., Narcotics Treatment Agency programs. Summary evaluation data (but not individual records) were the main source of information on these programs.

Many questions arose about the usefulness of these numbers, particularly since data collection procedures and practices had probably varied. An attempt was made to identify differences in clientele characteristics and data collection practices that would affect comparability, such as lengthy prescreening periods before a client would be officially counted as a client (this might screen out the less motivated before "counting" started).

d. Estimation of the likely effectiveness of each alternative. From the program evaluation of the existing county treatment programs and from other program evaluations that had already been conducted on several programs outside of Dade County, analysts estimated likely future performance factors for each treatment mode or program. They assumed that future performance would be the same as that in the past. Considerations included dropout (or the converse, retention) rates, percent graduated as rehabilitated, their likely rate of return to drug use, the percent of dropouts who were partly rehabilitated, and the various costs per client-month. From these data, and from estimates of the numbers of drug abusers felt likely to request treatment, the number of person-years essentially *heroin*-free, the number of clients rehabilitated (essentially free of *any* narcotics), and the program costs were calculated.

The number of person-years heroin-free was calculated for each alternative from three major components: (1) time period while the clients were in treatment; (2) the period from successful graduation until recidivism, if any; and (3) the length of time for dropouts who nevertheless had apparently been in treatment long enough to obtain some benefit. Note, however, that society and the individual might not value these equally since, other things being equal, it would presumably be better to be drug-free and self-sufficient in the outside community than constrained full-time to a therapeutic treatment community. In addition, it was necessry to distinguish those free of any of the hard drugs as opposed to those free of illicit drugs but still on some other narcotic, such as methadone. Analysts, however, did not attempt to apply different values to these respective conditions.

Because there was uncertainty about the proportion of persons who could be rehabilitated, based on the program evaluation findings, the final estimates of effectiveness showed a range of values rather than a single figure.

Step 5: Summary of costs and effectiveness for various program combinations. The analysts projected costs and performance for a period of five years for a number of combinations of treatment program expansions. This period was selected to permit sufficient time to reflect the effects of bringing in more clients and their longer-run disposition, including possible recidivism in future years. A period longer than five years was not felt to be appropriate, since the long-run effect of these programs was not well known. Exhibit A-4 shows the form of the output of these projections.

Step 6: Preparation of findings and recommendations. In addition to the findings of the type noted above and shown in Exhibit A-4, various other recommendations were made, as invariably occurs in analyses. These included recommendations to: (1) encourage treatment of addicts flowing through the criminal justice system, (2) attempt to discover why the backlogs for certain county treatment programs were low and to take action to try out ways to make them more attractive, and (3) improve coordination among programs and consider common sharing of certain activities, such as urinalysis, to reduce costs.

Impact of the Analysis

The county did not formally act on the specific alternatives for expansion. The analysis itself did not make major recommendations on specific treatment programs. This occurred partly because the estimated performance and costs of the residential therapeutic centers were quite similar.

However, the analysis and its recommendations on location and intervention of addicts processed through the county jail was one of the bases for the implementation of a treatment diversion program as a substitute for prosecution. Á future assessment using study methods is planned for reviewing county drug programs in the current face of reduced funding levels.

Miscellaneous Considerations

The drug abuse problem has been of considerable concern in state and local governments throughout the country. Great

Exhibit A-4. SUMMARY COMPARISON OF FIVE-YEAR
ESTIMATED PERFORMANCE AND COSTS FOR
THREE ALTERNATIVE PROGRAM MIXES TO
CURRENT PROGRAM*

Evaluation criteria	Current program level	Added costs, services, and performance		
		Alternative 1 (high cost)	Alternative 2 (medium cost)	Alternative 3 (low cost)
Costs	$7.6 million	+$15.9 million	+$10.3 million	+$5.8 million
Individual clients served	7,500-9,000	+9,300	+7,600	+6,200
Clients rehabiliated	unknown	+ 810	+ 580	+ 380
Person-years potentially drug-free	minimum of 4,800-5,300	+9,100-+9,600	+5,900-+6,200	+3,300-+3,600
Maximum cost per person-year potentially heroin-free	$1,600	$1,700	$1,700	$1,700

*Costs and performance of each of the three alternatives are in addition to the current program. Thus if Alternative 1 were adopted, the five-year costs are estimated to be $15.9 + $7.6 = $23.5 million; the person-years potentially heroin-free 13,900-14,900; and a maximum cost per person-year potentially heroin-free $23.5 million ÷ 13,900 = $1,700.

Exhibit A-4 (continued)

Program elements	Current program level	Added costs, services, and performance		
		Alternative 1 (high cost)	Alternative 2 (medium cost)	Alternative 3 (low cost)
Methadone maintenance	3 units, with total capacity of 500	+13 units with total capacity of 1,300	+8 units with total capacity of 800	+4 units with total capacity of 400
Habit reduction quick detoxification	none	+850 clients/year	+850 clients/year	+850 clients/year
Long-term residential therapeutic community (50 client capacity per unit)	4 units	+4 units	+3 units	+2 units
Short-term, small therapeutic residential community (20 client capacity per unit)	1 unit	+3 units	+2 units	+1 unit
Probation officers for surveillance	none	+11 units	+7 units	+4 units

Source: Marvin R. Burt et al., *Dade County Drug Abuse Treatment System Policy Analysis* (Washington, D.C.: The Urban Institute, October 1972), pp. ix-21.

controversy has arisen about decisions on the particular drug treatment methods to be employed. Individual treatment program staff have felt that their approaches and clients are unique, and that they cannot and should not be compared with others. Nevertheless, for a community or state with scarce resources, difficult choices have to be made as to which programs should receive what financial support. Even rough comparisons such as described above provide decision makers with relevant information on likely costs and performance.

In a complex analysis such as this, which involves many agencies (some private), special attention should be provided for actively involving agency personnel in collecting and analyzing cost and effectiveness data on their own programs. At the very least this will avoid misinterpretation of data obtained and it should help improve the quality and credibility of the study.

It would be highly desirable for such systems as drug treatment programs that the government undertake periodic evaluation and analysis and provide appropriate continuing data collection. Thus, if a similar analysis is attempted in, perhaps, another year, and if provision has been made for standardizing data collection and obtaining follow-up information, the analysis would be considerably easier to undertake and should provide estimates that are considerably more precise.

The importance of cooperation and review of agencies affected by the analysis was brought out clearly in this effort. The review of the early drafts of the report surfaced a number of critical issues. Had agency personnel participated as part of the analysis team, some of these problems might have arisen earlier and been handled better.

Appendix B
Two Illustrative Outlines of an Issue Paper

Outline Number One [1]

An issue paper is a written presentation that attempts to identify and describe the main features of a significant problem. It defines the problem, a first step in any program analysis. It does not provide the cost and effectiveness information that would be included in a program analysis.

The issue paper may stand by itself as a description of that problem area to provide an improved perspective of the problem. Preferably, it is used to set the framework, as the first phase of an in-depth cost-and-effectiveness analysis of the problem.

The issue paper should address questions such as the following:

A. *What is the problem?*

1. What seems to be the real problem?

2. What are the causes of the problem? To what extent are they known?

3. What specific population (client) groups are affected? (If other than the general public, identify their special characteristics, such as

---

[1]Adapted from The George Washington University, State-Local Finances Project, "A First Step to Analysis: The Issue Paper." PPB Note 11 (Washington, D.C., July 1968).

139

age group, race, income class, special needs, or geographical location).

4. What is the magnitude of the problem? How widespread is it now? How large is it likely to be in the future?

B. *Objectives and evaluation criteria*

1. Toward what public objectives should programs for meeting the problem be directed? Sought here are the *fundamental* purposes, not the immediate physical outputs.

2. How can estimates of progress against these objectives be made? Identify the appropriate evaluation criteria (measures of effectiveness). If these do not seem directly measurable, indicate the substitutes that might be used.

C. *Current activities and who's involved*

1. What other government agencies, sectors of the community, or other levels of government, in addition to this one, are attempting to meet the problem?

2. What activities relevant to the problem are being undertaken by this government? Identify each current program and, to the extent possible, provide current costs and estimated impacts, relative to the criteria in B.2. Indicate the number in each client group identified in A.3 and those currently being served. If possible, project these into the future, based on current planning.

D. *Political and Other Significant Factors*

1. Are there major political factors that seem to affect the problem?

2. Are there any unusual and significant resource or timing limitations?

E. *Alternatives*

1. What alternative programs or activities should be considered?[2] Describe the major characteristics of each.

F. *Recommendations for follow-up*

1. What is recommended as the next step? The Issue Paper should not normally contain *program* recommendations for choices among alternatives. But it should indicate what should be done next. Recommendations as to the timing and scope of follow-on analysis should be made, whether the analysis is to be of the "quick-response" or "in-depth" type.

2. What are the major data problems likely to be associated with an in-depth analysis? How might these problems be met in the short run and the long run?

Outline Number Two [3]

A.   Purpose of program: A brief statement of the purpose of the program being studied.

B.   Issue: A brief statement of the issue.

C.   Problem definition: Include in the definition the following items of information where applicable:

1. A definition of the problem and possible causes.

2. A review of existing state policy (specify statute or executive declaration) in terms of target groups, service levels and administrative approaches utilized.

---

[2]Though the issue paper should present an *initial* set of alternatives, this should not inhibit the formulation of new alternatives as the subsequent program analysis proceeds.

[3]Adapted from State of Virginia Commission on State Governmental Management, *Third Interim Report: Recommendations on the State's Budget Process* (Richmond, Virginia, December 1974).

3. Anticipated developments affecting the future direction of related programs including population, economic, social and similar changes.

4. The social impact on groups affected by the issue.

5. The fiscal impact of the issue, both existing and potential.

6. The roles of agencies, public and private, in relation to the issue or problem.

D.   Analysis of alternatives: Evaluate the alternative actions which the state might take in responding to the problem. Alternatives might be formulated based on one or several of the following approaches:

1. Alternative objectives—different effects to be achieved by government expenditure.

2. Alternative ways to achieve objectives—different outputs of government programs to achieve the same effects.

3. Alternative ways to carry out a program—different means of producing the same output.

4. Alternatives over time—different time spans for achieving objectives.

5. Alternatives among programs—alternatives or trade-offs among programs which have similar objectives.

6. Alternative methods of financing.

E.   Recommendation: Include in this section the rationale for selecting a particular alternative including a summary of the primary factors supporting the decision.

F.   Statement of financial impact of recommendation: Include in this section, as appropriate:

1. A statement of the budgetary costs both in terms of capital outlay and operating expenses for the next biennium and for each of the succeeding two biennia.

2. A statement of the proposed source of funding—whether from the General Fund or a Special fund, and if from a Special Fund whether the funding is anticipated from state or federal revenues.

3. A statement of any tax or fee revisions necessary to fund the recommendation.

4. A statement of the impact on the state's economy or a locality's economy.

G. Statement of legislation: If the recommended alternative requires legislation for implementation, a draft of the legislation is to be included in this section.

H. Implementation plan: Include in this section a proposed plan to implement the recommendation assuming plan approval by the General Assembly. State explicit objectives to be accomplished by specific dates.

I. Evaluation: State the methods of evaluation of results of the program services, including the information necessary for evaluation purposes.

Appendix C
An Illustrative Checklist of Technical Criteria for Assessing Program Analyses

Definition of Issues and Problems

1. Does the analysis clearly identify the specific problem being addressed?

2. Are the specific clientele groups that are involved explicitly identified? Are estimates made of the future size of each of these clientele groups?

3. Are appropriate evaluation criteria identified? Do these criteria cover unintended, as well as intended, effects? Do they cover negative occurrences as well as positive? If any of these effects were subsequently ignored in the analysis, were reasons given for their not being used?

4. Are estimates of the *future* need provided?

Alternatives

1. Are alternatives presented?

---

[1]Adapted from Marvin R. Burt, Donald M. Fisk, and Harry P. Hatry, "Factors Affecting the Impact of Urban Policy Analysis: Ten Case Histories," Working Paper 201-3 (Washington, D.C.: The Urban Institute, July 1972).

2.   If alternatives are presented, are they real alternatives and not merely added to be rejected out of hand?

3.   Are the alternatives specific enough to be evaluated?

Estimating Program Costs

1.   Are all appropriate costs included? Are employee benefits included, as well as direct salaries?

2.   Are possible costs of other departments or agencies, as well as the agency being considered, included? (For example, an increased police force might lead to additional jail and court requirements.)

3.   Are true incremental costs identified for each alternative? Does the analysis avoid arbitrary cost-accounting adjustments? For example, are fixed costs properly distinguished from variable costs?

4.   Are future costs included, as well as current costs?

5.   Are imputed costs distinguished from actual cost outlays? For example, are imputed dollar values for travel time saved distinguished from actual cost outlays?

6.   Are other scarce resources identified (in addition to dollars)? For example, is there likely to be a significant shortage of trained personnel needed to successfully implement the proposed alternative?

Estimating Effectiveness

1.   Is each of the appropriate evaluation criteria evaluated (even if only in a qualitative way) so that the objectives are adequately covered, or are some objectives and evaluation criteria neglected and only data used that are easily available?

2.   Are multiple measures of effectiveness used? Does the analysis avoid a premature combining of measures of effectiveness into a single index of effectiveness, thereby hiding individual measures?

3.   Are data on the measures of effectiveness provided for each relevant population subgroup?

4. Are likely changes in the mix (and "difficulty") of the clients to be served,· and in the environment in which the program will have to operate, considered in making effectiveness estimates?

Treatment of Uncertainty

1. Is there some indication of how accurate or inaccurate the key numbers and assumptions are?

2. Is some indication provided of how sensitive the study findings are to the major basic assumptions?

The Time Problem

1. Are relevant future costs and benefits estimated and their time periods indicated?

2. Do the estimates cover a long enough time period to provide a fair comparison among alternatives?

3. If discounting is used, are the undiscounted figures also presented? [2]

4. If discounting is used, are the proper caveats shown to indicate the considerable technical uncertainties as to the appropriateness of any given discount rate?

Selecting the Preferred Alternatives and Solutions

1. Are the costs and effectiveness estimates compatible with each other? That is, are they based on the same assumptions and data?

2. Are the cost and effectiveness estimates of each significant alternative summarized and presented together clearly?

---

[2]Discounting is a technique sometimes used to reflect the time value of monetary inputs. It has been used to represent the economic opportunity cost for removing funds from the private sector.

3. Do the analysts leave major value judgments to the political decisionmaking process?

4. If recommendations are made, do the results recommended follow from the analysis, or do they merely fall back upon unsubstantiated opinions?

Implementation Feasibility

1. Does the analysis imply any recognition of possible implementation difficulties? Does it consider the effects of likely implementation problems on the costs and effectiveness of the various alternatives?

Documentation

1. Is the report clear, concise, understandable, and usable by a decision maker? Does it have a reasonably brief, clearcut summary?

2. Are the assumptions clearly identified in the document? Can the reader understand how the analysis used data and translated them into cost and effectiveness estimates?

3. Have all affected agencies had the opportunity to review and comment on a draft report prior to formal issuance?

References and
Selected Bibliography

A. Principles and Techniques of Program Analysis

Burt, Marvin R., Donald M. Fisk, and Harry P. Hatry. "Factors Affecting the Impact of Urban Policy Analysis: Ten Case Histories," Working Paper 201-3 (Washington, D.C.: The Urban Institute, July 1972).

Davis, Robert H. "Measuring Effectiveness of Municipal Services." (Washington, D.C.: International City Management Association, Management Information Service (LS-8), August 1970).

Dorfman, Robert. *Measuring Benefits of Government Investments* (Washington D.C.: The Brookings Institution, April 1965).

Downs, Anthony. "How Cities Could Use Economists; Why They Don't; What To Do About It." *Public Management,* July 1971.

——————. *Inside Bureaucracy.* (Boston: Little, Brown and Co., 1967).

Fisher, Gene H. *Cost Considerations in Systems Analysis* (Santa Monica, California: The RAND Corporation, December 1970).

Georgetown University, Public Services Laboratory, "The Cost and Effectiveness Paper" (Washington, D.C., May 1971).

The George Washington University, State-Local Finances Project, "A First Step to Analysis: The Issue Paper" (Washington, D.C., July 1968).

——————. "The Role and Nature of Cost Analysis in a PPB System" (Washington, D.C., June 1968).

Gorham, William. "Rooting and Nurturing Better Decision Making in The Public Sector." Address to the American Association for the Advancement of Science, Boston, Massachusetts, December 1969.

Hargrove, Erwin C. "The Missing Link: The Study of Implementation." (The Urban Institute, July 1975, URI-12200.)

Harper, Edwin L., Fred A. Kramer, and Andrew M. Rouse. "Implementation and Use of PPB in Sixteen Federal Agencies." *Public Administration Review,* November/December 1969.

Harris, Robert. "The Implementation of Policy Analysis." Paper prepared for the New York City meeting of the American Society for Public Administration, March 23, 1972.

Hatry, Harry P. "Can Systems Analysis Be Institutionalized in Local Governments?" Urban Institute Reprint URI-10041 (Out-of-print), (Washington, D.C.: The Urban Institute, 1970).

_____. "Criteria for Evaluation in Planning State and Local Programs." Prepared for U.S. Congress, Senate, Subcommittee on Intergovernmental Relations, 90th Cong., 1st sess., July 21, 1967.

_____. "Overview of Modern Program Analysis Characteristics and Techniques." (Washington, D.C.: The Urban Institute, 1969, URI-10045).
_____, et al. *Practical Program Evaluation for State and Local Government Officials.* (Washington, D.C.: The Urban Institute, September 1972, URI-17000).

Hinrichs, Harley H., and Graeme M. Taylor. *Program Budgeting and Benefit-Cost Analysis* (Pacific Palisades, California: Goodyear Publishing Company, Inc., 1969).

Hirsch, Werner Z. *Program Budgeting in the United Kingdom* (Los Angeles, California: Institute of Government and Public Affairs, 1972).

Hitch, Charles J. *Decision Making for Defense* (Berkeley and Los Angeles: University of California Press, 1965).

Holbrecht, Herbert, et al. "Through a Glass Darkly." *TIMS Interfaces, the Bulletin of the Institute of Management Sciences* 2 (4), August 1972.

Hoos, Ida R. *Systems Analysis in Public Policy: A Critique* (Berkeley, California: University of California Press, 1972.)

International City Management Association. "Applying Systems Analysis in Urban Government: Three Case Studies." (Washington, D.C. March 1972).

Kimmel, Wayne A. "Planning, Analysis and Processes of Choice." Manuscript. (Cambridge, Massachusetts: John F. Kennedy School of Government, 1967).

Kraemer, Kenneth L. *A Systems Approach to Decision Making—Policy Analysis in Local Government.* (Washington, D.C.: The International City Management Association, 1973).

Larson, Richard C. *Urban Police Patrol Analysis* (Cambridge, Massachusetts: The MIT Press, 1972).

Lee, Douglas B., Jr. "Requiem for Large-Scale Models." *Journal of the American Institute of Planners,* May 1973.

Lee, Robert D., Jr., and Ronald W. Johnson. *Public Budgeting Systems* (Baltimore: University Park Press, 1973).

Lehne, Richard, and Donald M. Fisk. "The Impact of Urban Policy Analysis." *Urban Affairs Quarterly,* 10 (2), December 1974.

McCullough, J.D. *Cost Analysis for Planning-Programming-Budgeting and Cost-Benefit Studies.* RAND Publication P-3479 (Santa Monica, California: The RAND Corporation, November 1966).

McKean, Roland N. *Efficiency in Government Through Systems Analysis* (New York: John Wiley and Sons, Inc., April 1958).

Merewitz, Leonard, and Stephen H. Sosnick. *The Budget's New Clothes* (Chicago: Markham Publishing Company, 1971).

Mishan, E.J. *Cost-Benefit Analysis* (New York and Washington: Praeger Publishers, 1971).

Mushkin, Selma, and Brian Herman. "The Search for Alternatives: Program Options in a PPB System." The George Washington University, State-Local Finances Project (Washington, D.C., October 1968).

National Association of State Budget Officers, "A Survey on the Developments in State Budgeting: A Survey Conducted by the National Association of State Budget Officers Systems, Techniques and Data Committee." (Lexington, Kentucky, April 1975).

Pennsylvania, Commonwealth of, Governor's Office. "Program Policy Guidelines." (Harrisburg, Pennsylvania, August 1970).

Quade, E.S. *Analysis for Public Decisions* (New York: American Elsevier Publishing Company, 1975).

_____. "Cost-Effectiveness: An Introduction and Overview," P-3134. (Santa Monica, California: The RAND Corporation, May 1965).

_____and W.I. Boucher, eds. *Systems Analysis and Policy Planning: Applications in Defense* (New York: American Elsevier Publishing Company, Inc., 1968).

U.S. Department of the Interior, Bureau of Outdoor Recreation, *Assessing Public Recreation Needs.* (Ann Abor, Michigan, November 1974).

U.S. Environmental Protection Agency, *Evaluation of Techniques for Cost-Benefit Analysis of Water Pollution Control Programs and Policies.* Report of the Administrator of the Environmental Protection Agency to the Congress of the United States (Washington, D.C.: U.S. Government Printing Office, 1975).

Rivlin, Alice M. *Systematic Thinking for Social Action* (Washington, D.C.: The Brookings Institution, 1971).

Rosenbloom, Richard S., and John R. Russell. *New Tools for Urban Management* (Cambridge, Massachusetts: Harvard University Press, 1971).

Sackman, H. *Delphic Assessment: Expert Opinion, Forecasting, and Group Process.* RAND Publication R-1283-PR. (Santa Monica, California: RAND Corporation, April 1974).

Schultze, Charles L. *The Politics and Economics of Public Spending* (Washington, D.C.: The Brookings Institution, 1968).

State of Virginia Commission on State Governmental Management. *Third Interim Report: Recommendations on the State's Budget Process* (Richmond, Virginia, December 1974).

Steiss, Alan Walter. *Public Budgeting and Management* (Lexington, Massachusetts: Lexington Books, 1972).

Szanton, Peter L. *Analysis and Urban Government: Experience of the New York City-RAND Institute.* RAND Publication P-4822 (New York: The New York City-RAND Institute, April 1972).

_____. *Systems Problems in the City.* RAND Publication P-4821. (New York City-RAND Institute, April 1972).

The Urban Institute and the International City Management Association, *Measuring the Effectiveness of Basic Municipal Services: Initial Report* Washington, D.C., February 1974, URI-74000).

_____. "Improving Productivity and Productivity Measurement for Local Governments," four volumes (Washington, D.C.: The National Commission on Productivity, June 1972).

Winnie, Richard E. "Local Government Budgeting, Program Planning, and Evaluation." (Washington, D.C.: The International City Management Association, Urban Data Service 4 (5), May 1972).

B. Publications Containing Examples and Case Studies of Government [*Especially State and Local*] Program Analyses

Burt, Marvin R., and Louis H. Blair., *Options for Improving the Care of Neglected and Dependent Children.* (Washington, D.C.: The Urban Institute, March 1971, URI-60001).

_____*et al.* "Dade County Drug Abuse Treatment System Policy Analysis" (Miami, Florida: Office of the County Manager, Metropolitan Dade County, October 1972).

_____*Policy Analysis: Introduction and Applications to Health Programs* (Washington, D.C.: Information Resources Press, 1974).

Childs, L.S., *et al.* "An Analysis of Hawaii's School Health Screening Programs" (Santa Barbara, California: General Electric Company TEMPO, June 1969).

Fisk, Donald M. *The Indianapolis Police Fleet Plan* (Washington, D.C.: The Urban Institute, October 1970, URI-50002, out-of-print).

Fort Worth Research and Budget Department. "The Use of Police Patrol Cars by Off-Duty Patrolmen" (Fort Worth, Texas, 1970).

Fromm, Gary, William L. Hamilton, and Diane E. Hamilton, *Federally Supported Mathematical Models,* NTIS-PB 241562 (Washington, D.C.: Data Resources, Inc. and ABT Associates, Inc., June 1974).

Goeller, Bruce F., *et al. San Diego Clean Air Project: Summary Report* (Santa Monica: The RAND Corporation, December 1973).

Hausner, Jack, and Warren Walker. *An Analysis of the Deployment of Fire-Fighting Resources in Trenton, New Jersey* (New York: The New York City-RAND Institute, February 1975).

Illinois Economic and Fiscal Commission. *Water Resources Management in Illinois: Program Review* (Springfield, Illinois, January 1974).

International City Management Association. "Applying Systems Analysis in Urban Government: Three Case Studies." (Washington, D.C., March 1972).

Kakalik, James S. et al. *Improving Services to Handicapped Children.* Report prepared for the Department of Health, Education, and Welfare, Office of the Assistant Secretary for Planning and Evaluation (Santa Monica, California: The RAND Corporation, May 1974).

Ko, Stephen C., and Lucien Duckstein. "Cost Effectiveness Analysis of Wastewater Reuses," *Journal of the Sanitary Engineering Division,* December 1972.

Metropolitan Dade County, Florida. "Metropolitan Dade County Alcoholism Treatment Policy Analysis." (Miami, Florida, April 1974).

Metropolitan Government of Nashville-Davidson County. "A Search for Alternatives: An Analysis of Program Options in Five Selected Issue Areas." (Nashville, Tennessee, July 1970).

Novogrod, R. Joseph, *et al.* "Ambulance Service." *Casebook in Public Administration* (New York: Holt Rinehart and Winston, Inc., 1969).

Pennsylvania, Commonwealth of, Office of the Budget, Division of Program Audit. *Program Audit Report on Vocational Training in Pennsylvania State Correctional Institutions* (Harrisburg, Pennsylvania, October 1970).

Popovich, Michael L., Lucien Duckstein, and Chester C. Kisiel. "Cost-Effectiveness Analysis of Disposal Systems," *Journal of the Environmental Engineering Division,* October 1973.

Public Services Laboratory. "Lead Poisoning in Children: The Problem in the District of Columbia and Preventative Steps," (Washington, D.C., Georgetown University, 1971).

Rosenbloom, Richard S., and John R. Russell. *New Tools for Urban Management.* (Cambridge, Mass.: Harvard University Press, 1971).

Spiegel, Mathias L., and E. S. Savas. "Emergency Ambulance Service for the City of New York." Office of the Mayor, Office of Administration, (New York, March 8, 1968).

Thompson, Quentin, "Assessing the Need for Residential Care for the Elderly," Quarterly Bulletin No. 24 (London: Greater London Council Intelligence Unit, September 1973).

The Urban Institute. *The Struggle to Bring Technology to Cities.* (Washington, D.C. 1971, URI-70001).

Willemain, Thomas R. "The Status of Performance Measures For Emergency Medical Services," Operations Research Center, Massachusetts Institute of Technology (Cambridge, Mass., July 1974).